HOW to make a MONEY machine

a beginner's guide to making money and keeping it

Wink & Julie Grisé

Lothian
BOOKS

Thomas C. Lothian Pty Ltd
132 Albert Road, South Melbourne 3205
www.lothian.com.au

Copyright © W. & J. Grisé 2004
First published 2004

National Library of Australia
Cataloguing-in-Publication data:

Grisé, Wink.
How to make a money machine.
ISBN 07344 0651 7.

1. Finance, Personal. 2. Saving and investment.
3. Investments. I. Grisé, Julie. II. Title.
332.02401

Cover design by David Constable
Cover illlustration by David Dickson
Text layout by Amanda Griffin
Printed in Australia by Griffin Press

Contents

WE love MONEY

Men are not ashamed to proclaim their undying love for it. Women sing its praises. Kids know all about it.

Money.

Some of us save it, but we all spend it. Like dieting, we budget, swearing off the big purchases, unnecessary expenses and late-night shopping. We *will* make do without frivolous luxuries! Yet like diets, our budgets often suffer, especially around the holidays when it's easy to bend to pressure and buy just 'a little something extra'... with more accessories sprinkled on top.

Money.

The government prints it. Guys named Rocco in abandoned warehouses print it. Why shouldn't regular folks like us be able to print it?

Well, we can't print money, but we can create it—not just earn it, but have money that will spawn more money. This book will help you with your money, whether you just want to manage it better or create new wealth. It will teach you how to build your own money machine and show you how to work smarter, not harder.

1

It's easy

Most of us look at the prospect of improving our wealth and think it's all too hard. 'You have to be born rich, or have gone to a good school and started working at it right away.' Maybe that's true in some ways, but it sounds a little like an excuse, doesn't it?

The truth is, there's no complex formula to make yourself better off. (There's also no single secret.) The hardest part of increasing wealth or just managing your money better is actually getting out and doing it! This book will help. It's a no-bull guide. That means we don't sugar-coat the truth. We tell it like it is, even when the news is painful. What you read might shock you. It might surprise you. But as we uncover the secrets of making a money machine, you'll find many surprises especially pleasant.

About getting rich

1   It's not *magic*.
2   There's no *single formula*—everyone's situation and goals are different.
3   It's not *complicated*, but it does take effort.
4   *Act* on what you learn.

It's not magic

You've got to make it happen, and that doesn't mean buying lottery tickets. (It's a recorded phenomenon that over one-third of lottery winners go bankrupt!) There are plenty of hair-brained schemes, scams and self-delusional plans. Many people become 'seminar junkies', paying heaps of their hard-earned cash to go to every money-making seminar and course. Why do they do it? Are they really increasing their knowledge and financial education, or are they just hoping to find the one true secret that will make them a success? They seem to believe that one of those courses will deliver a magic formula. Well, we can assure you, all it will do is make the seminar people rich.

The simple truth is, all you have to do is follow tried-and-true advice and put a bit of effort into making money ... and the sooner you begin, the sooner you can reap the rewards. Even so, it's never too late to improve your financial situation.

There's no single formula

You have to make your own personal recipe for wealth. You might be trying to find the answers in the formula your neighbour Ralph used, but everyone's path is different. Ralph might have started with small investments and grown them into some substantial money, or maybe he took over a small business and bought other businesses. Whatever he did, he took advantage of opportunities. You will have different opportunities. That's okay, you'll find your own path. Some steps on your own path might be more difficult than Ralph's, but some will be easier.

It's not complicated, but it does take effort

You don't have to be a genius or get two degrees in business at a big university.

Making money is actually very simple. It just requires work, and we'll show you how to choose the work that's most efficient. It can be as simple as selling biscuits and charging more than you spent to buy them; or even better, buying cheap raw materials and baking your own biscuits, so that your profits increase. All the principles involved in making money are easy to understand.

The catch is that you will have to work to turn ideas into profit. And it usually won't happen instantly.

Sometimes it may seem like watching grass grow. But it *does* grow!

You don't need buckets of money to start. Even if you're on welfare, one commodity you probably have is time. Use it.

Act on what you learn

You have to actually *use* what you learn. There's an old joke about doctorate scholars: A person with a PhD may know everything about the history, construction and operation of mousetraps, but probably couldn't design one, build one or use one. (Apologies to all PhDs out there.)

Literally everything in life comes down to two basic questions:

1   What do you want?
2   How hard are you willing to work for it?

In this case we're talking about money, but these same points apply to making lunch, studying at school, asking someone out for a date, anything. Ask yourself what garbage will you put up with and why.

Another way to look at it (maybe more optimistically) is: What is the ratio of profit to effort? Most people want to do as little as they can for the most reward. And guess what? Anything else is just not logical. You could get out of the car in the cold rain and open the garage door by hand, or you could spend a little money once and install a remote door opener.

Think about the reasons you want more money. Is it to increase your financial security, or do you want extra money for travel and hobbies? Maybe you just want to become stinking rich. Would you rather continue drilling holes in sheet metal at your nightshift job and keep on dreaming of being better off or would you rather work at increasing your wealth? If you've got to expend energy and make an effort no matter what you do, then you might as well be working towards a goal.

This book will help you get started. We'll tell you about some important concepts and facts and we'll show you how you can design your own way to riches. Now let's get started!

MONEY Practices

A lot of people live from pay cheque to pay cheque. They have a minimum amount in the bank, then they deposit their pay cheque, withdraw it all as soon as they can, and spend it all. 'Yippee! I've got $600 cash!' Not true! What they really have is 1/52nd (or if paid fortnightly, 1/26th) of their year's pay. But they also have many expenses: fixed, variable and unexpected.

To continue in a cycle like this is to *plan to be poor*! You can never get ahead, never conquer or at least manage your expenses. Every week will always be a struggle. Obviously, more money would help, but aside from free money falling into your lap, just changing how you handle money will help. You need to build up savings, and to plan for all your expenses. Which brings us to …

A money plan

Money plan, spending plan, spending schedule … these are all names for the same thing: setting down a plan to manage your everyday and long-term expenses. *This is the single most important financial step anyone can make.* It's the foundation for everything else. We can't stress this enough.

Governments and companies use spending plans. Big and small businesses use plans. Anyone who needs to know where their money is going uses a plan.

You might *hate* the thought of making and using a plan. Maybe you absolutely despise planning and keeping track, and you feel limited by a plan.

Get over it. You absolutely need a money plan.

The only alternative is to waste your money and not be able to buy the things you need and want. *A plan will get you out of the financial doldrums and into financial heaven.*

Look at people around you. Some will be struggling with money, others managing well. The people struggling aren't planning. The people doing well *are* planning.

Maybe you've been getting along without a plan. You've either been extremely lucky (and luck will run out), or you have a rough plan in your head.

So, we agree you need a plan.

By now you may have figured out that 'plan' is another way to say ... *budget.* Don't panic!

'Budget' is a bad word for some people. It may conjure up images of misers living on a severe money diet, *but a budget doesn't limit your spending.* The amount of money you make in a year limits your spending. If you earn $30 000 a year, you'll have $30 000 to spend whether you use a budget or not.

With a budget you'll be able to figure out how much you can spend on fun things after you pay all your bills. Better to budget than to spend all your money on a new car and stereo, only to find you don't have enough left for food and rent. The people who spend like this live in a fantasy world, thinking they should grab the toys now while they've got cash and worry about expenses later.

Your budget doesn't have to be overly-detailed or too rigid, but the better the plan—and the better you manage it every week—the easier it is to spend wisely. You won't be wondering how you'll pay bills or when you can have a treat. You'll know, because it's written down.

Let's create a simple budget. (You only have to do this once, then make minor adjustments.) Add up all the money coming in. That's *income*, the total you have to work with. Include wages, government benefits, investments, etc. Looks nice, doesn't it? If only you had this to spend each week. Hey, hang on, you do!

Next comes the cruncher, *expenditure*. Break it down into three categories: fixed (bills that are the same amount each time they are due, like rent/mortgage, insurance, council rates, school fees, etc.); variable (bills you can control, like electricity, phone, water, food, etc.); and optional (usually luxuries or items not necessary for living).

Now, add up the cost of each expense for the whole year and divide by 52 weeks. For example, you might spend $800 a year on electricity. It might vary from bill to bill, but you can add them all up and get a rough average. (If you haven't kept records, check your account activity or call the company and ask.)

Electricity

Jan–March	$157
Apr–Jun	$240
Jul–Sep	$220
Oct–Dec	$183

$800 ÷ 52 weeks = $15.38 per week

This is the most difficult and important part of setting a budget! Once you've worked out how much to put aside, you won't suffer any bill blowouts.

Add up all the weekly expense totals. That overall total

is how much you need to put aside each week for your bills. End of discussion.

Here's a simple budget. The figures are just an example, yours may be more or less.

SIMPLE BUDGET (WEEKLY)	INCOME
Main income earner	
Take home pay (wage after taxes)	$600.00
Second income earner (part-time)	
Take home pay	$200.00
EXPENSES	
Fixed	
Mortgage/rent	$280.00
Car reg ($400 year ÷ 52 weeks)	7.69
Insurance (house & car ÷ 52 weeks)	27.00
Variable	
Electricity ($800 year ÷ 52 weeks)	15.38
Water ($400 year ÷ 52 weeks)	7.69
Phone ($700 year ÷ 52 weeks)	13.46
Petrol	35.00
Food	130.00
Optional	
Video/DVD	5.00
Alcohol	20.00
	$541.22
	$258.78 left over

Hopefully you have some money left over each week. An amount of about $260 each week is $13 520 per year. Do you have that much sitting in your bank account? If you do, read ahead and learn to invest. If not, where did the money go?

Morning coffee and lunch might take $30–40. That reduces your $260 to $220. Add pocket money for kids, drinks after work, a movie, a trip to the hardware store, new clothes, and you're soon down to just a few scraps, if not zero. It goes fast when you're not watching. So watch!

Don't forget to budget for those indulgences. There's no point in having megabucks saved if you never get to enjoy it! Something inexpensive and simple can be a real treat if you know you can afford it because you've budgeted for it. It's all about moderation, but you should take moderation in moderation too!

Often overlooked categories to include

Entertainment You're just fooling yourself if you don't include this. Videos, eating out, magazines, sporting event tickets, etc.

Miscellaneous Make sure you cover one-off rare items like driver's licence or passport renewals. You should also think about how much you spend each year on birthdays and Christmas.

Bank fees These are regular and definite, count them in; the bank does!

Car maintenance Oil changes, tune-ups/servicing.

Car emergencies Brakes and blown fromulators. By pre-saving at least a little bit, you'll be better off when a problem hits. If you make a year without problems you've got 'free' money.

You should now have something that looks like this (we've added extra for the maintenance and emergencies we mention above):

INCOME	$800.00
EXPENSES	
Fixed total	329.67
Variable total	233.98
Optional	
Video/DVD	5.00
Alcohol	20.00

Meals out	40.00
Kids' pocket money	20.00
Magazines	15.00
Movie (whole family)	40.00
	$703.65

$96.35 left over

Now, that's a bit more realistic. Make sure you cover everything; there's no point kidding yourself. What you can't do without, budget in. What you can do without or reduce is what you need to work on.

Make sure you add a 'contingency' category to protect yourself from hidden expenses and price rises, like Aunt Zelda clocking up a $200 call to Upper Kumbukta West. Corporate and movie budgets usually set the contingency to 10 per cent of the budget. If your expenses come to $700 a week, add $70.

Now comes the tricky bit. Each time you get paid, put aside the money for the expenses. Here's the real trick: *only spend it on those expenses.* Don't spend the $15.38 for electricity on an extra lunch out just because the bill isn't due yet.

Simple, wasn't it? You'll never have to worry about finding money for bills again. You've just learned a secret, pat yourself on the back.

So now you have a budget, what do you do with it?

Stick to it! It shouldn't be painful. If it is, reorganise your spending. You can make up a budget that you *can* stick to and still enjoy life.

Any left-over money isn't a bonus. We mean that. It's not a joke. This is how you will increase your wealth. Use the money left over to earn more money. If you really want that plasma TV, buy it out of your investment income, not your savings. In this example you will put aside around $700 a week to cover everything. The $96.35 left over isn't spending money either because you've included your spending money for videos, magazines, etc in the budget.

Now that you're having a good look at what you spend, are there things you can do without? Are you spending too much on something you shouldn't be? You might think you can't afford a new car, but if your old one is actually costing you more than a loan and maintenance would, then getting the new car might be the best thing to do.

If you're spending $50 a week on going to the movies, can you wait a few months and rent the DVD?

Places to save (without being a miser)

You may shudder when you see this list, thinking you can't possibly cut back on any of these 'essentials' or try these ideas. That's fine, we all have different priorities.

Food shopping

Eliminate eating. It's expensive, time-wasting and just plain fattening. (Just kidding.) When appropriate, buy the no-name brands. For many items, quality is the same in an expensive brand as it is for a no-name brand. Take rice. A grain of rice is a grain of rice, no matter what brand it is.

Check the labelling on packages and compare big brands to no-name brands. Sometimes you'll find they share the same manufacturing plant. Items like laundry detergent are often just as good in the no-name brands.

The smile discount

You can get a really good deal sometimes by just being nice. Seriously! Imagine you work behind the counter in a retail store and some miserable, nasty person comes in and is mean, abrupt and unfriendly. Are you going to mention discounts? But if someone is nice and friendly, and acknowledges you, you're inclined to be nice.

Smile, chat with the clerk and ask 'Is that your best price?' or 'Is there a discount for cash?' If it doesn't work, at least you had a pleasant shopping experience. Not every store or assistant can give discounts, but it's worth a try.

In some countries, haggling is the only way to shop. If you shop at a market you're almost expected to haggle. It can be lots of fun, too. But be warned, never demand a discount or push too hard.

Game, set and price-match

Most large retail stores or chains will price-match a competitor. Some will discount beyond the match. This can be handy if you don't want to travel to East Overshoe to get a bargain. Most stores will need proof of the competitor's price. Remember, though, it's 'apples for apples'. The deal has to be identical and in stock. (It isn't fair to the store otherwise.)

Compare

It's definitely worth the time and effort to compare prices. For repairs and large purchases, get at least three quotes and go for the middle one (too cheap is as bad as too expensive — it can be a nasty shock to find out you've paid for inferior parts). Compare prices on food shopping, too. You'd be surprised at how much you can save. Sometimes supermarkets in the same chain but in different areas will have vast price differences. Try to shop in a lower income area. The price differences on individual items can add up to $50 or more in your weekly grocery bill.

Cast your net

If you have a computer and you're online, let your fingers do the work and check company websites. Sites like 01FREE (www.01free.com.au) offer discount vouchers to shops and restaurants. The web offers many free deals, such as music (MP3 files) and freeware/shareware computer programs. You can even get TV guides emailed to you for free, rather than buying a magazine or newspaper. Some companies offer free samples of their products. Go surfing and see what you can get.

A lot of people are afraid of Internet shopping because they don't feel safe typing in their credit card details and sending them off into the electronic netherworld. You don't have to worry. As long as the site you're on has a secure area (a padlock or key comes up in most browsers), your credit card details are very safe. Secure sites encrypt the information (convert it into a complicated code), which makes it more secure than an EFTPOS machine! Giving your credit card number out over the phone or writing it on a form is actually more risky.

If the company is big and well-known you shouldn't have anything to fear. If you're still unsure, try a phone order, or print out a form from the site and fax or mail it.

Bargain hunting

There are plenty of places to shop to get a better deal. Keep your eyes and ears open for warehouse sales, factory outlet sales or scratch and dent sales. You can sometimes save up to 50 per cent. If you need to buy furniture or appliances, will second-hand be just as good? Check the trading papers, go to garage sales or auctions. There are shopping guides available to buy at newsagencies that list all the factory outlets and bargain warehouses.

Bulk up

Buying items in bulk can save you a small fortune. Some supermarkets offer bulk discounts, but you'll usually find bulk-buys at cash and carry stores, with things like wine clubs, or buying through network marketing companies like Amway. If you live near a bakery or abattoir you can often buy direct for much less.

Don't fall into the 'per unit' price trap, though. Buying 100 widgets might lower the price from $2 each to 50 cents, but instead of buying three for $6 you've got to spend $200. Make sure you can use all the product, especially before any expiry date, and that it's something you do actually use and would buy normally. (There's no point in getting a great deal on pet food if you don't own a pet!) If you only save $1 each on 10 items but it'll cost you $5 in wastage, is it worth it?

Petrol

Always fill up early in the week (or the cheap times in your area). The prices often go up from Thursday to Sunday, to catch weekend drivers and those who wait for pay day to fill up. There is definitely a pattern, despite the claims of no price fixing by the petroleum industry. (Don't blame the petrol station; they only make about 5 per cent profit. The rest is split between the oil company as profit, and the government as tax.) You can save about $250 a year by buying when petrol is cheap. And don't buy the super high octane stuff unless you have a high performance car — the slight increase in quality is not worth the huge increase in price.

Real money eaters

Mobile phones

People love them. So handy, so much fun! But it's easy to get carried away. Instead of just using a mobile when needed (for example, when away from a 'landline' or regular phone), people tend to use them all the time. Some mobile providers even have 'convenient' calling plans to help out: just one flat rate. An outrageous 37 cents per 30 seconds, billed in 30 second intervals! If you talk for 31 seconds you pay for 60 seconds. You can call halfway around the planet on a discount carrier landline for 10 to 16 cents per minute, but calling across town on a mobile is going to cost you more than 50 cents a minute!

Mobiles are really just two-way radios, and they shouldn't cost more than a landline to use. There's no reason for a 'flag fall' or call-connection fee, either. The fact is, you pay for the convenience of a portable phone. You pay right through the nose! The price is based solely on huge profits for the telephone companies, and the numbers are so big they're almost arbitrary.

What can you do? You *can't* give up the mobile, it's become a part of your business and personal life. Okay, but use your mobile wisely. Don't be a slave to the mega corporations.

Why not use a prepaid plan? It can seem less professional but it's a great way to keep you aware of how much you spend. You need to look for a company that offers one-second billing, one cent or less per second, no flag fall (charge for connecting each call), and prepay recharges that last a long time. Compare plans and weigh all the features against each other.

Some monthly plans offer free or cheap calls at certain times. If you use the phone at these times, go for it. If you find you don't talk to many people between midnight and five am, then it might not be a good deal for you.

Watch out for the ads offering phones for '$0'; they're misleading. They give the distinct impression you're getting a phone for '$0', but in reality, it's $0 *upfront*. You're actually paying for the phone with monthly payments, *in addition* to the monthly call plan, which often does not include calls! A new phone and a simple per-month plan could cost you over $1000 a year. Were you paying that much before you had a mobile?

Some plans say '$20 a month with $20 worth of calls!' Sounds great. But with a high call charge, that $20 may only give you 25 short calls, or about one call a day for a month.

SMS/text messages can be a bit of a trap, too. They average 25 cents each, though they can cost more. Send four or five messages and you've spent a dollar. Do that every day and you've spent $365 on probably meaningless messages. Many mobile users send 20 messages or more a day. That's $1200 a year! Use them sparingly. Some calling plans include a few text messages in the monthly price. But remember, you're still paying for them.

A last piece of advice about mobiles: follow the plan. Choose a network provider carefully. Consider the calling plan to be a set of instructions on how to get the most out of the company. If they offer free or discount calls at night, then take advantage of that. 'Free after X minutes' can be a good offer, but you pay a lot for those first few minutes.

Cigarettes

We won't lecture you on the evils of smoking, just the economic realities. At $10 per pack, the average light-to-moderate smoker spends $3000 a year on smoking! That's a lot of money to hand over to rich corporations because you've become physically addicted to their product.

Break your addiction. Stop making tobacco companies rich.

Quitline: 13 48 48
Cancer Council: 13 11 20

Gambling and pokies

This is going to hurt some people. Big shock coming up here. Hotels and gambling establishments are in business to make money. And they do a great job of it. In South Australia alone they net (after payouts) about $543 million a year from people playing the poker machines. That amount increases every year, up from $186 million when the machines were first introduced outside casinos. And that's just South Australia. Numbers like that mean it's a profitable business. If it's profitable for those gambling establishments, how can you get rich playing pokies?

You can't.

Before pokies were electronic, they had a mechanical lever and were nicknamed 'one-armed bandits'. An accurate description. Pokies promise to pay out 87.5 per cent. That figure sounds wonderful, but the truth is, if you walked in with $100, you would walk out with only $87.50. The pokies take, on average, 12.5 per cent of your money.

Of course, people play hoping that they will be the ones playing the machine when it pays off with other people's money. And sometimes it happens. But the numbers work against you. You might win $250 after a few spins. You probably won't, but you might. You might even win in the thousands. You probably won't, but you might. If you think it's harmless entertainment that has a chance of putting some extra 'fun' money in your pocket, then go have a good time. Just make sure you budget a small amount to risk and don't go over that amount. Most importantly, don't be disappointed if you lose it all.

Some safety tips

1   Budget a small amount for entertainment only; do not go over this amount, and do not withdraw more money if you lose all of it.

2   If you win, don't think that you can keep winning.

3   If you win big, don't think that you can win big again.

4   Know that other than an occasional lucky big jackpot, it is impossible to get rich playing pokies. If you have great skill and a lot of luck, you might get rich playing blackjack, but not pokies. (Just look at all the people who lose their house and job, and spend $180 000 playing pokies trying to win $5000. An Adelaide man embezzled $20 million over eight years to cover his gambling addiction, which included pokies.)

Gambling hotline: 1800 060 757

Christmas

Ahhh, the time of the year when we ... wait in long queues, battle traffic and shove shoppers. The season of shopping. If you celebrate Christmas you know it's very expensive. Even if you plan to keep it simple, Christmas can easily get out of control. There's probably Christmas cards (plus postage), there's holiday food (fattening and expensive), maybe a tree, decorations and, of course, presents.

We're not saying you should eliminate Christmas, but you might think about which expenses are worth the money. Take one quick stroll through a shopping centre at Christmas and it becomes obvious that it's no longer a holiday, but a forced shopping season. We're bombarded with and assaulted by advertising, not to mention retailers insisting we spend as much money as possible. To not spend is to shirk your duty. Buy this useless flinglehopper! Buy two widget cleaners! Spend spend spend!

When you're a child, Christmas is a fun and magical time. It takes centuries to arrive, and even though the day is over all too quickly, it's a Big Event. There's school holidays, and it seems to be Christmas for a week. But as an adult, it can easily become a burden of credit card debt and a day of family arguments, all over in a flash.

Thoughtful gifts and activities can be more enjoyable, and they'll save you heaps. Get the kids involved in making cards for all your relatives and friends. It's fun for them and cheaper for you, and Grandma will love it! If you buy $30 gifts for fifty people, that's $1500! Give them a bottle of wine or beer, chocolates, a homemade basket of treats (get the kids involved again), or a movie ticket voucher. They'll still love you and you'll save plenty. Let them know your budget and ask them not to spend too much on you. You'll hear the sighs of relief from miles away.

Make sure your kids are aware of your budget (or Santa's if they're little). They can't have a pair of those $300 sneakers, plus the $500 skateboard and a DVD player. Let them know they can have one of the big items and they'll only get one or two other small presents if they do. Give them the money limit and have them draw up their list from that. They'll soon figure out their own priorities, and you'll be surprised at how practical kids can be when given the opportunity.

> A Christmas Club account can help with your
> budget, too.

Buying a car

Car advertisements on TV often try to sell you on a 'feeling', rather than showing you the features and benefits of a particular model or brand. The executive driving at high speed in exotic locations may look nice on TV, but it doesn't help you make an informed decision about what's right for you.

Research is the key to any good deal. Ask yourself what

kind of car you need. Something small to get you around town? Will you be going long distances on weekends, or will you need room for camping gear and several mates? Make a list of what you want and need in a car, then try to find a brand and model that fits the bill.

Your list of car luxuries and utilities is a personal choice, but consider these features:

Power steering Power steering gives much better control in car parks and on roundabouts.

Airconditioning Studies show that the load an airconditioning system puts on your engine (thereby reducing fuel efficiency) is roughly equal to the drag caused by having your windows open, so you might as well go for air. But if you're buying an older car, make sure the airconditioner takes the new environmentally friendly gas, otherwise you'll need to have a new system installed, and that can be expensive. However, keep in mind that most airconditioning systems have to be re-gassed every year or so, no matter what type of car you have.

Automatic transmission It's very cool to shift a manual, but in bumper-to-bumper traffic your clutch foot can stiffen and become a weak, gnarled sausage. If you do a lot of city or heavy-traffic driving, think long and hard about getting an automatic.

Don't buy new

There's no easy way to say this … new cars are a rip-off! They've got warranties and are stylish, but they lose their value very quickly. The average mid-size car selling new for $30 000–35 000 will drop $15 000 in value in just 12 to 18 months! That's a decrease in value of over 40 per cent. New car manufacturers don't want you to think about this. We've bought both new and used cars, and we'd never buy factory-new again.

You can save a lot of money by purchasing a car that's one to two years old. They are still under warranty, they have low kilometres on the odometer, and they look new. Cars like this are not rare or hard to find; many companies buy or lease fleet cars and then swap them for new cars every year or so, and if you take the time to look around you can scoop up a deal.

The average driving distance for a car is 20 000 kilometres per year, so make sure the cars you look at have travelled the average number of kilometres or less. Beware of ex-rentals and cars that have been driven hard, as they'll have higher kilometres and possibly more engine wear.

Another way to save is to buy last year's model. The new models come out in August/September, and dealerships are anxious to offload the 'old' stock. Last year's model is still a new car, but it will sell for less than a current model. You won't save as much as you would if you bought a car that had been sold and driven, but then again, you'll have a car with almost no kilometres on the odometer.

Where to buy

Once you have made your list of must-haves, get online and use the web. Websites like www.carsales.com.au have powerful, easy-to-use search features that can show you a wide variety of cars. When you've selected a few targets, go and test-drive them! There's nothing like actually sitting in the car and getting a feel for comfort and visibility. When we bought our last car, we originally thought we'd buy Brand A/Model X, because it was very stylish and fitted our requirements, but when we test-drove the car we hated it! It felt cramped, there was no visibility, and it drove like a truck. And don't be afraid to try each major brand. Brand loyalty clouds the mind, and you could be ignoring your perfect car.

For safety we recommend buying from a car dealership, because you have some recourse if you have problems with the car. Some dealerships are better than others, and you'll get to know the reputations of those in your area. All the cars on the lot, new or used, should be clean and look new. Good presentation shows that the dealer cares about the car and the sale. Be wary of dirty, ill-repaired cars.

Make sure the car you are interested in has been inspected. Some dealerships have certification programs, usually connected to your state's automobile club (such as the NRMA, RACV, RACQ or RAA). If the dealer has no such program, or if you think the guarantee offered on the car is inadequate, have an auto club inspect the car. This usually costs about $150, but you get a full written report on the condition of the car, highlighting any existing or potential problems. Some problems can be repaired as part of the purchase deal.

Tyres are usually not considered in a used car sale. The tyres may have been cleaned with 'tyre black' and look new, but it's important to check the tread. Some tyre wear is common in used cars, and you'll probably have to resign yourself to buying new tyres in six to 12 months, but make sure the tyres aren't bald.

Sales tricks and tips

Car salespeople get paid on a commission or quota basis, and they will do almost anything to get you to buy the car the day you drive it, including pressure and rewards. Most consider it a lost sale if you're 'just looking'. Do not be swayed by sales talk. Ask yourself if the car really meets your requirements, and if it is a fair price. And, of course, test-drive it.

You can also beat some of their tricks by treating a car purchase like an investment. (But remember, it's *not* an investment: a car never appreciates in value.) As when you are investing, do not be emotional. If your dream car is too expensive or sold to someone else, don't panic: you *will* find the right car.

To get the best deal, attack a sales person at their weakest and look for a car when they are desperate. Go shopping three to seven days before the end of the month, late in the week, in the afternoon. They will be close to their monthly quota deadline at that time, and they will be more likely to bargain.

When you feel close to making a final decision, a salesperson might sweeten the deal to try to push you over the edge. Often their tactic is to say something like, 'If you take it right now, I think I can persuade my boss to knock off $1000.' They are trying to make you think they are your personal helper, fighting for the best deal, just for you. They fill in all the paperwork but have to 'run it by the boss' for final approval; they go into the back room and 'fight for you'.

What they really do is have a quick coffee with a middle manager, then come out looking disappointed and say the boss will only knock off $500. You've gone this far and will probably agree — it's okay if you do. The dealership has probably given you their best price in order to cement the deal, so if you like the car and your budget can handle it, buy it. It can be fun to walk away at this point, though. You never know if they'll go lower. But remember, they have to make *some* profit.

Trade-ins

If you have an existing car, you will probably get a little money for it if you trade it in at the dealership. Dealers have to refurbish the trade-in car and resell it, so don't expect them to offer you a lot of money, and don't let a trade-in make or break a good car deal.

Finance

Get pre-approval from your bank. You'll know exactly how much you can spend, and you won't waste time looking at cars you can't afford. If you own a house (or are paying off a mortgage), try to get a loan linked to the mortgage, as you can often get a much lower interest rate this way. The process will take longer because your house will need to be re-valued, but it can be well worth the trouble. Whatever you do, don't sign up a hire-purchase agreement with the dealership — their interest rates will be far higher than the bank's.

Insurance

Insurance often seems like a waste of money — until you need it. It's best to just grin and bear the pain, and pay for adequate insurance. It's important to at least be covered for damage to other people's property in the event of an accident. With litigation becoming the new favourite pastime, it's possible to lose your house and income if you're sued for hitting an expensive luxury car. You should also have comprehensive insurance to cover damage to your car, so you don't need to worry about finding the money to pay for repairs to or replacement of your car in case of an accident that is your fault.

Agreed value

Many insurance companies will let you insure your car for an agreed value of the car, for the life of the car, rather than adjusting the insurance each year as the car depreciates. Insuring for an agreed value costs more, but you won't notice much difference in your payments, and it can save you an enormous amount of money later.

For example, say you insure your car for an agreed value of $25 000. Eight years later your car would normally be worth, say, $12 000, but because of the agreed value, you can still get up to $25 000 from the insurance company if it is damaged or written off (damaged beyond repair, or damaged more than the car is worth). Very helpful if you suddenly have to get a new car!

BaNKiNg

Saving

One of the most basic money skills is saving. It's smart, and with a little bit of effort and a system, it's doable. But remember: as healthy and necessary as it is, you can't get rich by saving! The old advice 'a penny saved is a penny earned' is an outright lie. You're just putting money away from a limited income, not increasing your money. But more on that later in *Increasing Your Wealth*. For now, know that saving is always important.

Losing and not losing

You should also know the difference between losing and simply not gaining. If your car, the money-eating machine that it is, drops a vital part on the highway, you have an unexpected repair bill. It's a bit like being robbed. You've suddenly lost money.

But what if you have a $100 discount voucher for

Widgets R Us, and can't use it before the voucher expires? Have you lost $100? Has $100 been erased from your wallet? No, you just didn't gain the savings you would have if you'd bought a widget. A subtle but important difference!

Bank accounts

To function in modern society, everyone needs a bank account. Life is too inconvenient without banks. Stuffing money under your mattress is not safe and could lead to back trouble. Most employers deposit money in employee accounts electronically; without a bank account it's difficult for them to pay you. There's no escaping banks.

Some people think banks work like this: A happy bank manager merrily skips to greet us, shakes our hand and promises to defend our money to the death. To thank us for this privilege, the bank will pay us interest! Oh, and here's a free toaster and a chance to win a trip for two to Fiji.

How banks really work: There's no bank manager in sight because they're all too busy trying to make a profit and can't be bothered with our paltry little deposit. If you do catch them skipping it's because they're so happy counting the penalty fees the branch pulls in from overdrawn accounts and other violations. Even a small bank, across all branches, can pull in over $50 000 in fees *per day*. This doesn't count the exorbitant fees banks charge for simple services that cost them almost nothing: $15 to issue a bank cheque, $5 for a money order, $15 to convert foreign cheques to Australian dollars, etc.

The banks may smile at each individual depositor, but they laugh out loud at the collective cash they can use to lend out and invest. A bank is in business to multiply its money. It operates the business by providing services to customers who deposit and borrow. The customers obtain a service, but the bank makes money.

Basic accounts

Isn't it funny that any bank account that isn't a cheque or business account is called a 'savings' account? It should really be called a 'spendings' account! To make saving easier it's best to have two separate accounts, one for true savings and one for bills. Or, if fees are high (and you can be disciplined), divide one account into two on paper: a 'spending' part and a 'saving' part. (There are a lot of good and affordable computer programs that make this easy.)

It's important to do your research when choosing the account that's best for you. There are many different types of accounts, and each bank has variations. We've provided some general information from three big banks below, but be aware that details may vary from bank to bank.

Have as few separate accounts as you can manage in order to minimise fees. Shop around and find the best deals.

Savings

Most banks have a basic savings account. It doesn't have bells and whistles (no ATM card, no cheque book, no overdraft facility) but it also doesn't have high fees. This is a good account to use as a true savings account, because no ATM card means no dipping in. Shop around the credit unions, too; they often have better deals for 'fee-free' accounts. Credit unions can be a trade-off: low fees for limited branches and services.

Passbook and statement

Generally the standard bank account is divided into two types, Passbook and Statement. The accounts are the same but the reporting method is different. A passbook is a passport-sized document and every time you make a deposit or withdrawal, it is recorded in the passbook as a way of keeping track of the transactions.

Banks try to discourage passbooks. It's more expensive for them to produce the passbooks and more difficult to manage, as each transaction requires the book to be updated. Since you hold onto the book, the bank has no control. Passbooks can be lost, creating a security risk for you and the bank. Be aware that some banks may charge more to transact on a passbook account, but there are also extra fees involved with a statement account.

A statement account uses a periodic statement or list of your transactions. A statement is mailed to you weekly, monthly, quarterly or annually, depending on the bank and your choice. If you lose your statement or need a replacement, banks often charge $5–7 *per page* for a duplicate. If you want a statement more often than they like to send them, you'll also be charged. Overall though, a statement account is usually the better option.

Christmas Club

If you have trouble saving, look at a Christmas Club account. Not only are they good for helping you to save for Christmas, but you can use the same system to save for other items. A Christmas Club account works like this: every week you deposit a set amount of money into the account (or it can be deducted from your pay automatically). At the end of the year, just before Christmas, you get the whole amount to spend for Christmas shopping. It's forced, disciplined saving and it works well for many people.

You can do the same thing yourself to save for other items. Some employers even give the option of putting aside extra money for superannuation or social clubs.

Term deposit

Term deposits are a type of investment account. They pay much higher rates than an ordinary savings account, because the bank has your money for a set period of time and they can use it longer term for investing or lending. The interest rate will depend on how much money you've invested and for how long. The more money you invest and the longer the term, the higher the rate.

If you're a terrible saver (or good spender, depending how you look at it) and want to be able to put some money aside for a larger purchase like a holiday or that plasma television you've been drooling over, and you have a timeframe, then think about a term deposit. Terms vary depending on the bank, but usually you must deposit a minimum of $1000 for three or six months. Some banks let you top up by adding money. The more you put in the more interest you'll earn.

Some term deposits let you access the funds more regularly. They usually offer various terms ranging from one month to five years, and pay the interest either on set intervals (say every three months) or when the term is due (*rolls over*). If you invest for say three months, every time you roll over you can add more funds or take some out. And the longer the term, the higher the rate.

Say you win $10 000 on a scratch ticket. Rather than spending it, you could pop it into a term investment for two years and watch the interest compound the investment (this means that you earn interest on your interest, as each time it's paid your investment is greater). At the end of the term you might have, say $12 000, and can buy a bigger plasma TV! Or, if you're really smart, you can get the normal-sized TV and invest the interest to earn more money for your next purchase.

Automatic teller machines (ATMs)

ATMs are robot tellers. You can use them at any time of day or night and withdraw up to $800 (or more) in one day. While it's possible to deposit and transfer money between accounts, most people use them for withdrawals.

Most people are now familiar with how to use an ATM, but we'll go over it here anyway. You start by inserting an ATM card into the ATM and use a keypad and computer screen to enter your Personal Identification Number (PIN) as a security password. This is like a key; guard it well. If someone steals your card they can't use it without the PIN. If they try to guess and hit random numbers, they usually only have three attempts before the ATM captures the card. The chances of any human guessing the correct four-to-six digit number in three tries are pretty slim, because there are around one million combinations! It's virtually impossible to guess, unless you use an obvious number like a birth date. And of course you would never keep your PIN written down near your card, would you?

When choosing a PIN, keep in mind that any PIN is four times more likely to begin with the number 0. And the numbers 1 and 5 are used more often than the other digits. Choose wisely.

Banks want you to use ATMs because they cost less to run. Human tellers are expensive to maintain; they demand holidays, lunch breaks, toilet breaks, set work hours etc. ATMs just require a cash refill and some routine maintenance, plus a little electricity. Banks still charge transaction fees for using ATMs, but the charge is far less than going to a human teller. Many banks also offer a number of free transactions per month. Beware: it is easy to incur lots of fees by overusing ATMs.

There are ATMs at shopping centres, attached to banks or just inside separate bank lobbies. They are also found in service stations and pubs. Everywhere. But not every ATM is on the same system as your bank. Chances are you can use your card in almost any machine in the world, but you will be charged an additional fee if you use your card in a 'foreign' system. By 'foreign' we mean not necessarily a machine in another country, but a competing teller machine. For example, you can use your Dingo ATM card at any Dingo teller machine for a small fee (maybe you are allowed a few transactions a month free). You can use it in Acme teller machines, but you'll be charged an extra $1.50 or more per transaction.

ATMs are useful, but they can be a trap. If you take out all your wages when your pay cheque hits your bank account, then you're tempted to spend all your money. If you use the ATM to only take out what you need each time you buy something, you're less likely to spend all your money at once. You don't have to carry lots of cash, and you are more likely to spend only what you need. Be careful though, that you don't go over the maximum number of 'fee-free' transactions per month.

Cheques

A cheque is an IOU — a promise to pay later. It's a low-tech way to function without carrying cash. Very handy, but there are problems for both the cheque writer (payer) and the cheque bearer (payee). Cheques take three to five days to 'clear', in other words, to transfer the money from the payer's account into the payee's account.

All cheques are filled in roughly the same way wherever you are in the world. There is a place to write who the cheque is for (payee), the date, the amount in both numbers (1–2–3) and words (one–two–three). And there's a signature space. In Australia we can also stamp or write 'not negotiable' across the face, so that the cheque can only be cashed by the payee and not some crim who might have stolen it. You can also mark a cheque 'Account Payee Only', which means it *must* be deposited into a bank account in the payee's name only.

Just because a cheque has been written doesn't mean there's actually money in the account to cover it. When you miscalculate how much money you have and write a cheque for more money than you have in your account, it 'bounces' or is returned, marked 'insufficient funds' or 'refer to drawer' (the person who drew the money or wrote the cheque). The person you wrote the cheque to is very unhappy, because they don't have their money and because their bank has charged them a fee for the bad cheque (around $10). You're very unhappy because your bank charges you a fee too (around $35).

Important! Even though it takes three to five days for a cheque to clear, that doesn't mean you have those days to get the funds into your account. So don't write a cheque and put money in later! When you write a cheque you must have money in your account. (It's technically part of your agreement with the bank when you open a cheque account.) Here's why.

Say on Monday you write a cheque to Jane for $100. You only have $75 in your Dingo Bank account, but you know you'll be getting some money in the next day or so, no worries.

Jane immediately deposits the cheque into her account at Acme Bank. Acme instantly credits Jane's account with $100, but puts a hold on it until they can verify the cheque is good, meaning Jane can't withdraw the $100 for three to five days.

That night, Acme Bank exchanges the cheque with Dingo Bank and Dingo Bank debits your account $100. But you only have $75 in there. Uh-oh. Your Dingo account shows –$25; Jane's Acme account shows +$100.

The next three to five days is for Acme to talk to Dingo to sort out paperwork, and to allow Dingo to say 'Whoa! There isn't enough money in the account to honour the cheque! Cancel!'

On Tuesday Dingo quickly reverses the cheque out of your account so you're not overdrawn and sends it back to Acme with the 'not enough money' message. On Wednesday Acme has learned you don't have enough money in your account at Dingo. They tell Jane that she's deposited a bad cheque, and charge her a penalty. Dingo tells you that you don't have enough money to cover the cheque, and charge you a penalty. So on Monday you gave Jane a cheque and on Wednesday she finds out that it's a dud — there's the three days! (That's the minimum possible time, but it could be longer if the banks are in different states.)

Let's say you have $500 in your account when you give Jane her cheque for $100. But $450 of that money is from a cheque you received from your Aunt Dorothy. Aunt Dorothy's cheque hasn't cleared yet, so you still can't write any cheques on it.

To avoid this situation you decide to give Jane her cheque, but you'll put Thursday's date on it instead of Monday's. That way the cheque can't be cashed until Aunt Dorothy's money is clear in your account, right? Wrong!

Aside from the fact that it's technically illegal to write a date in the future or post-date a cheque, it won't guarantee that the cheque won't be cashed or credited before that date. The date is mostly a convenience; it doesn't get read by the computer in the bank, only the amount does. It's entirely possible (and likely) for the cheque to still be put through the system without the date being picked up. It's really only the eagle eye of a teller that will save you.

How to balance a cheque account

Balancing your cheque book, or maintaining an accurate listing of your account transactions, is very important. Otherwise, you'll never know how much money you have. Or worse, you'll think you have more than you do. Here are a few things to remember:

1   When you write a cheque, make sure you record the transaction right away. Otherwise you'll forget.
2   Include any bank fees.
3   Match your statement to your cheque book stubs.
4   Go through line by line and look for errors.

Alternatives to cheques

If you just want an easy way to pay bills, we suggest taking advantage of the various electronic systems: EFTPOS, direct debit, Internet banking and BPay, phone banking or credit card.

EFTPOS

That's a long-winded way of saying 'debit card'. EFTPOS stands for Electronic Funds Transfer at Point Of Sale. It is like a cheque, but instead of handing over a paper IOU with the money taken out of your account later (debited), an EFTPOS transaction is electronic and instant. The money is electronically deducted from your account and transferred to the payee's account instantly. (Actually, the information is exchanged instantly and verified later during the day by computer.)

ATM cards are used for EFTPOS sales. Just swipe your card and enter your PIN, as you do at an ATM. You can access your savings or cheque accounts in this way.

Always check the total on the screen before hitting the OK button. Sometimes the sales clerk can make a mistake keying in the amount, and you could accidentally OK a $5000 pencil. While it might be sorted out later, it's a hassle.

Sometimes the ATM or EFTPOS system can go offline. If it's partially down you are issued an offline voucher and the transaction will go through later. You have to sign an offline voucher, which is basically your promise to pay.

Sometimes an EFTPOS machine won't dial out, but usually on the second or third try the transaction does go through. It's a good idea to keep all the receipts that say 'error' or 'transaction cancelled', because occasionally you can be accidentally charged twice and keeping a record of all the faults will help sort out the problem.

Direct debit

Direct debit is convenient and automatic. You sign an agreement to let a creditor (a company you regularly owe money to, such as an insurance company) access your bank account to take out money to cover your bills. They still mail out your bill, but instead of your having to arrange to pay it, they just tell you what date they'll draw the money from your bank account. It all happens automatically; no queues, no hassles, no worrying or forgetting to pay the bill on time. All you have to do is make sure the money is in the account, and if you've been budgeting you'll always have enough for your bills.

Some direct debit transactions have a small fee, but it is comparable to the cost of a postage stamp, and it sure beats standing in a queue!

Internet banking and BPay

If you have a computer and an Internet account, take advantage of Internet banking. Most banks are web-ready and charge very small fees, or nothing at all, for Internet banking. You can check on your accounts and transfer money between your accounts or to someone else's account at any time, making it much easier to manage your money.

If you haven't reached the point of absolutely needing a computer, or can't afford one along with the Internet fees, you can still take advantage of Internet banking features. For only the cost of a local phone call you can usually do all the same things with phone banking. Instead of a screen, you just use your phone keypad and follow the voice prompts.

BillPay (BPay) is like any Internet banking, but it's even easier. Participating companies (utilities like power and gas, banks and even many shops) all have a BPay biller code. You just make a quick funds transfer from your account to theirs by entering their biller code and your reference number, usually your account number.

The clearance on these transactions is similar to that of cheques. It's quicker because there's no paper to transfer, but there's still an overnight electronic data exchange between banks before the transactions are processed. So don't wait until the very last second to electronically pay a bill — it's a good idea to pay a day or two before the due date just to be sure.

Credit cards

Credit cards are even better than cheques because they allow you to spend now and pay later. While a cheque is all the necessary paperwork you need to actually debit your account, a credit card is a two-part promise: first, to have a credit card company pay your bills for you right away; and second, a promise that you will pay back the credit card company later (usually in 30–55 days). If you can't pay back the debt in 30–55 days, you can pay part of the debt every month, plus interest, usually about 16 per cent.

Isn't it fantastic to have this little piece of plastic? Unlimited wealth tucked away in your pocket? You can buy that new lounge suite, stereo system or gold-plated toilet. Whack that puppy down on the counter and worry about it later. The bank doesn't care what you buy, and you don't even have to pay it back straight away, only a little each month. You don't even have to apply to a bank and suffer through the application process. Department stores encourage you to use their own cards, little plastic pots of gold. How can you say no?

Of course you can see some dangers here. Convenient, yes, but also potentially disastrous! Credit card companies love it when people charge up huge debts and can only afford to pay the minimum monthly payment. The minimum is usually the interest on what you owe plus a tiny bit of the *capital*, or what you actually spent. If you spend up big, the credit card company is essentially guaranteed regular profit from you for years. Paying only the minimum repayment means you'll almost never pay off the debt.

But credit cards are almost a necessity in the modern world. If you want to buy anything online or via mail order, you almost *have* to have one. They're also handy for an emergency, like when Great-Great Aunt Velma in Upper Kumbuckta West is dying and you have to visit her before she goes (to make sure you get into the will …). Credit cards are needed for deposits when hiring cars, equipment etc. A credit card proves you have a legal relationship with a bank and can be forced to pay if you steal the item you're hiring, or pay for damage if you break it. If you pay a cash deposit you could possibly steal a car for essentially a hundred dollars cash.

The best way to deal with credit cards is only to have the cards you *need*. It's very easy to accept the fifteen different cards you get offered or can obtain, but you really only need one. If you only have one it's easier to maintain. You can set a set limit on it that you know you can handle, and there's only one set of fees and interest to worry about.

Sure, some stores or companies offer discounts if you have their card, but sometimes you have to spend a certain amount each month. Is it really worth that $5 discount if you have to spend $1000 to get it?

Some of the frequent-flyer cards require you to spend around $80 000 to get one free air ticket worth a few hundred dollars. Now that's an expensive flight! You also may have to use *their* card to make the purchases, so they get the interest as well as your business.

If you can live without the advantage incentives, then forget the store cards and go with the banks and credit unions. The interest rates are lower and they won't give you what you can't handle. The special discounts on the store cards may not work out to be much of a discount when you take into account the higher rates, which are often 25–30 per cent.

> Many stores will charge extra for purchasing with
> a credit card, to get back the transaction fees
> they are charged by the banks.

If you really must have more than one card, be careful and watch your budget. You can reduce your limit on each card so that the combined total limit is an amount you can safely manage. Or you can pay off all your sundry cards with your main card each month, and stick to the limit on your main card. If you already have 27 different cards, don't panic. Many banks are quite happy to take them off your hands and combine them into either one card or one personal loan.

There are a few things to stick to when using a credit card:

1   Know your limit and don't go over it.
2   Make sure you pay off as much as you can each month. Don't just pay the minimum, you'll never pay off the main principal that way.
3   When you budget your credit card payments, make sure you budget in the interest and any annual fee.
4   When you're thinking of purchasing on a credit card, think, 'Do I really need this item now, or can I wait and save up for it?' Weigh in the extra cost of the interest you'll pay for it, and see if it's still worth it.

In addition to interest, most cards have an annual fee, usually $25–50. The fees can vary depending on the way the interest is charged. You can choose to pay interest straight away on purchases — for this some banks will charge no annual fee — or you can pay the annual fee and have 30–55 days interest free. You need to look at your own spending habits and see which works best for you.

Another feature of credit cards is that you can draw a cash advance, which is like a mini loan up to your credit limit. This is great to know in case of emergencies. But be careful — you pay interest on cash advances straight away, regardless of whether you have interest-free days on your card or not. If you need money immediately, look at a personal loan or overdraft. The interest rates will usually be lower, and set repayments make them easier to manage. (See *Mortgages and loans*, page 46 for more info on a loan.)

If you're smart and a good budgeter you can take advantage of the 55 days interest-free on your credit card.

You can pay for everything on your card, such as groceries, bills and expenses, without paying interest for almost two months! In the meantime you can leave your earnings in your bank account earning interest. If you have a mortgage, the money could be put into your mortgage account, thus reducing the interest you have to pay for that period. We'll discuss more about mortgages later.

> If you lose your card or it's stolen, call your bank and cancel the card immediately! Otherwise you may be responsible for charges to the card. You don't want to pay for a thief's trip to Europe. Many banks and credit card companies have policies to protect the cardholder, but it's important to cancel the card instantly.

Here is a brief rundown of the major credit cards in the market.

VISA & MasterCard

These are true credit cards. You don't have to pay the full amount right away; you can choose to pay a small portion plus interest. They are both widely accepted around the globe (22 million locations and 700 000 ATMs for VISA, 29 million locations for MasterCard). You can get a card either directly from the company or through a bank. Deals vary, but these are the 'meat and potatoes' cards — popular, simple and easy to use. Cards issued by CitiBank usually offer an extra security option: your colour photo on the card, so merchants can tell at a glance if someone is using a stolen card.

BankCard

This is an Australian credit card. It was introduced in 1974 as a joint effort of the major Australian banks. It's for use in Australia only.

American Express (AMEX)

AMEX is a 'charge card', which means you can use it instead of cash, but you must pay the bill in total in 30–55 days (there are some exceptions). Think of an AMEX card as a delayed EFTPOS card in a way. It's not offered through banks, just directly from American Express. There are some drawbacks to AMEX; so many in fact, that it's a wonder they're used at all: the annual fees are high, the card costs retailers more to use than other cards so prices are higher, and the card is not widely accepted.

Hmm … costs a lot, not as widely accepted, and you have to pay the full amount monthly. What are the benefits again? Actually, there are some for travel and discounts, but you really need to have a lot of cashflow to take advantage. AMEX is aimed at wealthy and corporate buyers, so the retailers try very hard to sell their AMEX customers more things at higher prices. And the AMEX customers usually go for it.

Diner's Club

This is another charge card, and you have to cough up the cash in 30 days. Believe it or not, this is the original credit card, dating back to the 1950s. It's not widely accepted, but does offer rebates on purchases. You'd think that after 50 years the idea would have caught on and they wouldn't have to entice users with rebates … There are variations, but the way it works is roughly similar to AMEX.

Debit cards

Debit cards are exactly what they sound like — they are the opposite of credit cards. With a credit card you get a line of credit, allowing you to make purchases and pay the bank back later. A debit card looks, feels, and acts like a credit card, but instead of using the bank's money, you use your *own* money.

They are really just like a bank account: you have to have the money in your account before you can spend it, and you access that money with your card. For those of us who have trouble handling a credit card but would still like the convenience of one, debit cards can be a good alternative.

Overdrafts

An overdraft is sort of like a loan, but instead of borrowing a set amount, you have a limit similar to a credit card. Generally people use an overdraft as an alternative to a small personal loan. Businesses use overdrafts to pay for business expenses and buy stock when money is tight. They pay off the overdraft when they receive money for their goods or services, which helps maintain *cashflow*.

Overdrafts are set up like a normal bank account, but allow you to overdraw your account by a set amount. Say you have $1000 in your bank account and an overdraft limit of $2000. This means you can withdraw up to $3000. The bank will charge you a set interest rate on the amount that you overdraw, and perhaps monthly or transaction fees. The interest rate is usually better than a credit card and comparable with personal or business loans, sometimes even lower.

Overdrafts are a little less dangerous than credit cards, as they are more like personal loans. You have a set repayment amount which covers both principal and interest over the whole limit, rather than just a minimum monthly payment over what you have spent. This ensures that you can and will repay the whole amount over a shorter period.

You can set up an overdraft to help with large bills, use the funds for temporary investment opportunities with a quick return, or just to make sure you have some funds available in an emergency. You can also use it like a business does. Say you wanted to have a small hobby business making and selling cookies. You can purchase the raw ingredients using the overdraft, bake and sell the cookies, then pay off the overdraft with the sales, keeping the profits for yourself.

There are also *reducing overdrafts*, which reduce your limit each time you make a repayment. This forces you to repay the overdraft over a period of time, much like a personal loan. These are great for one-off purchases, and usually offer much better rates than financing or using a hire–purchase plan.

Lay-by and rent-to-buy

You've walked into the local electrical retail store and spotted that huge plasma TV mounted on the wall. There's no way you can afford it, but they've got a great rent-to-buy or hire–purchase deal. You only pay a small deposit now and make a small payment each month. It's yours to take away right now! What a deal! Right? Wrong!

If you've ever been tempted to rent-to-buy, do the maths first. They usually fail to mention anything about interest rates, or if they do it's 'interest-free for 12 months'. They're lying. They don't charge you interest like a bank does, they just have a 'repayment plan'. If you crunch the numbers you'll find that after you add up all the repayments, surprise surprise, you could have bought the item outright for much less. Always check the original purchase price and compare. It's usually *not* a great deal. If you really, really want the item, then either save up for it (pretend you're making those repayments and put the money aside until you have the total) or use another payment method that gives you more control.

The same goes for lay-bys, especially those that hold the item until you pay it off. If you can't afford to buy something then and there, then you quite simply can't afford it, full stop. Don't go into huge debt just because a store makes it easy for you. If you really, truly need something, save for it.

Mortgages and loans

Why do I want a mortgage?

Owning a house saves you money. You might not think so when you consider how expensive houses are and how much they cost in maintenance, but it's true. Rent money is burned up and you get nothing tangible in return. Mortgage payments mean you actually own a piece of your house. The mortgage money you've spent can often be re-drawn (more on that later). And in the end you own a house. You can sell it, or you can borrow more money against the house. But when you're done paying rent, you own nothing.

Here's a secret: the average rent payment is the same as a mortgage payment!

The catch is that you need a deposit to get a mortgage. A bank won't loan you all of the money, and a deposit can be $10 000–20 000 or much more. What do you do?

You can start with a simple, small house and work your way up. You won't need much of a deposit for a small house. You can also take advantage of a builder's 'no deposit, house and land' package. In a few years, when prices are up and maybe your income is up, you can sell and get something bigger. Do this until you approach your dream house.

You can also buy insurance (see *Mortgage insurance*, page 55) so you won't have to save such a large deposit. And you can get a HomeStart loan — this loan is usually not a wise choice (pay less up-front, but heaps later), but it can get you started, and if the numbers work for you, it might be better than renting.

Banks for the money

A mortgage can seem like an act of charity from your bank. The bank actually buys your house for you! You would have to save up for decades to get one lump sum like that. The bank just asks that you pay the loan back in pieces over 25–30 years! For this they charge a little fee (*interest*).

Don't feel too bad for banks. That 'little fee' of interest adds up. A $100 000 loan at 6.5 per cent interest per annum (p.a.) or per year is not just $6500. Over 30 years it's $130 000 in interest, plus the original loan. You borrowed $100 000 and ended up paying back about $230 000.

The two biggest banks in Australia regularly post annual net profits of $2,000,000,000.00. (That's two thousand million, or two billion.)

It's official

The Reserve Bank of Australia (RBA) sets official interest rates. The RBA is a bank for banks, and helps set economic policy. The bank board meets and looks at various indicators to see how the economy is going. If there's no growth and things look bleak, they vote to lower the lending interest rate. They hope this will stimulate loans, which will in turn stimulate business and building. If the loan rate is low, why not buy or build a house? Regular banks take the official rate and tack on a small profit, from a fraction of a per cent to a few per cent.

Fixed versus variable loans

A fixed rate mortgage has its interest rate set for either the whole life of the loan or just a portion of it. A variable rate means that the interest changes with the rate set by the bank (which is based on the Reserve Bank rate). For example, Dingo Bank may be offering a variable rate of 4.00 per cent. But a few months later, the Reserve Bank changes the official rate to 4.25 per cent. Dingo then increases its rate to 4.75 per cent, which gives it a bit of profit.

It's most likely that you'll start off with a variable rate at a 'honeymoon' or very low rate for one year, and then have the option of continuing variable (at a slightly higher rate) or switching to fixed for a set time. Variable is great when interest rates are low, but when they begin to rise you pay more. If rates go too high you may not be able to afford your payments. The fixed rate option is usually available in one-to-five-year blocks. The fixed rate is slightly higher than the variable rate, but it's guaranteed for that set period of time. If rates drop or rise, you're still locked in to the rate you fixed.

This is one of those difficult decisions: fixed or variable. There's no right answer, just advice to help you maximise efficiency and minimise risk. You'll kick yourself if you lock in at a high rate and then rates drop to almost nothing, but you'll definitely smile if rates rise.

As with most decisions, it's probably best to aim for somewhere in between or do a little of both. When you start your loan, take advantage of the variable honeymoon rate. When it ends, if rates are generally high, or look as if they will rise, you might fix for just a short period, maybe one to three years, and go back to variable later.

What banks look for in a borrower

When you apply for any kind of loan the banks look for indicators that you can pay back the money easily.

Character

If you turn up at the bank looking like a wino who sleeps in the gutter, a bank will be less likely to accept that you're trustworthy and can repay the loan. Always act and dress as if you are going for a job interview. The classier you look, the more likely they are to trust you with their money. It's only common sense.

Banks also look at employment. If you've been working at the same job for a while it's more likely you'll remain employed and be able to repay. The same goes for where you live. If you have lived in houses for less than a year, banks think you move around a lot. They wonder if they'll get their money back because you might just wander off. They like boring and stable people.

Credit check

The bank may also perform a credit check on you. They'll get details of your credit history from the Credit Reference Association of Australia (CRAA), including any defaults you might have (loans and bills you didn't pay). Any loan that you've applied for in the past will also show up, even if you didn't get the loan. So if you've been to ten banks for a loan and this bank is the eleventh, they'll know about it and wonder why you've been declined by ten other banks. Late bill payment may show up too. Before you apply for a loan, make sure any outstanding debts have been paid and that the payee has marked your credit reference as 'paid'.

It's a good idea to get a copy of your credit report before you go to a bank for a major loan, so you can have any odd things fixed. The CRAA has become BayCorp, and they will give you a credit report for a small fee (www.baycorp.com.au).

Ability to repay

The bank will ask you to summarise your income and expenditure. (This is where budgeting comes in handy!) Be honest here, for your own sake as well as the bank's: there's no point getting the loan only to find that you can't make the repayments. Emotions and wishful thinking mean nothing; cold numbers mean everything. And keep in mind that banks have a formula for guessing what you spend. They know you can't feed a family of five on $50 a week. No matter how much you allocate, they use base average formulas to work out what expenses you might have.

One way to prove you can repay is to have a consistent savings history. If you can show that each week you put aside the amount required for the repayment plus some extra money, then the bank can see that you can make loan repayments.

These checklists and procedures may make banks seem mean, but remember, they're in business to make money, not give it away. Whether it's fair or not, it's how the system works. Instead of thinking of the requirements as a handicap, think of them as precise instructions on how to get money.

Identification check

Most banks use a checklist of official documents to prove you are who you say you are. For their purposes, each document is valued at a certain number of points. To prove your identity they require documents to the value of 100 points. Here's a simplified list of documents, and the points each one is generally worth. Each bank is different; this is a guide only to help you prepare.

DOCUMENT	POINTS
Passport	70
Citizenship certificate	70
Birth certificate	70
Known customer (at least 12 months)	40
Known customer (at least 36 months)	100
Written reference from another bank	40
Written reference from another customer (who has been identified under these documents)	40
Driver's licence	40
Public service ID card	40
Social security card	40
Tertiary education card	40
Employee ID card	35
Membership card	
— club, union, professional body	25
— educational institution	25

Usually a driver's licence and a birth certificate are enough.

Now that you've fulfilled the bank's requirements, how about getting them to satisfy yours ...

Things you want in a mortgage

There are many variations when it comes to mortgages, and some banks have wildly different ideas. There's no escaping fees completely, but they do vary depending on the bank. Usually, what you gain on the roundabout you'll lose on the swing. One bank may offer, 'No Application Fees!' but the interest rate is higher. One might have a great interest rate, but they charge a monthly fee. The best way to compare loans is to look at the bottom line. What is the total amount you will end up repaying over the entire life of the loan? You may have to pay a $600 application fee for one loan, but if it ends up saving you an extra $1000 over the life of the loan because there are no other fees or it's a lower rate, then it's a good deal.

It's unlikely that you'll find everything you want in *one* loan, so determine what the most important features are and find a loan that offers those things. Generally, don't worry too much about one-time fees. Worry more about recurring fees and expenses.

Don't just take the bank's word for things; make sure you have all the facts and don't be afraid to have them spell it out in plain terms. If there's something about the loan you don't understand, ask!

You can use a mortgage broker to help you find the right loan. They can do the hard work and show you the features and benefits of different loans, or *products* as they call them. They can assess all the fees and charges and interest rates for you. Mortgage brokers don't charge you; they usually get a commission from the banks. But choose a broker carefully. They should:

1   Be unbiased (do they get the same commission from each lender?)
2   Have formal qualifications
3   Offer a variety of lenders (10–15)
4   Spell out reasons for recommendations
5   Not encourage you to borrow more than you can afford.

Interest rate calculation

In the past, loan interest was calculated on the 'maximum monthly balance'. For example, if in January you owed

$90 000, and you made a repayment of $300 on the 3rd, your new balance would be $89 700. But you would still be charged interest on the $90 000 for the full month, even though it was only $90 000 for three days!

Today most banks offer loans with daily interest. That sounds a bit harsh, but it actually works for you: any time you make a repayment, the interest is recalculated on that reduced amount immediately. Extra payments have even more impact. For every dollar you repay, you're being charged a little less interest each time. Make sure this is how interest is charged on your loan.

Repayment frequency

Half-monthly and true-fortnightly repayments sound like the same thing, but they're very different. Half-monthly payments (on the 1st and 15th of each month) mean you'll make 24 payments in the year, two each month over 12 months. But if you make true-fortnightly payments you make 26 payments in the year, because each month has more than 28 days. You won't even notice those two extra payments, but they make a huge difference to the loan. Often you'll shave about one year off. Ask your bank to do a comparison for you. You'll be surprised at how much you can save, so make sure you ask for true-fortnightly payments.

Fees

Fees are tricky to nail down. Some banks call their fees by different names. One bank may advertise a zero or no application fee but they'll whack you with an administration fee instead. Get a summary from the bank of all the fees associated with the loan. Aside from the usual application fee, there may also be an administration fee, government duties (stamp duty, mortgage registration, etc.), valuation fee, progress payment fee, mortgage guarantee insurance, monthly fees (most likely if the interest rate is fixed); the list goes on. There may also be other fees attached to the loan over its life, such as early repayment fees, break costs (if you repay more than a set amount during a fixed rate period) and mortgage discharge fees.

Re-draw facility

Some loans let you make extra payments and then allow you to take the money back if you need it. Of course, you won't want to — it reduces any saving you gain from making extra payments. And banks don't make it easy to re-draw. They usually charge a fee ($25–30), make you apply, and then take a few weeks to get you the money, but it's handy in an emergency.

Voluntary repayments without penalty

Voluntary extra repayments will shorten the length of your loan. Find out if you can make them without being penalised. This is usually only a problem if the loan is fixed; most banks let you make some extra payments before making you pay penalties. Find out what that limit is and what the charges are if you go over it. The charges are called 'break costs', because you are 'breaking' a contract with the bank. (They have most likely borrowed your money from the Reserve Bank at a certain rate, so when you mess up the contract they have to pay the Reserve Bank.) The charges can be quite nasty, even in the thousands of dollars. The formula for estimating break charges is very complex and can really only be calculated by the bank. The fee will be approximate until the actual day you do the deal.

Line of credit

If you have a line of credit, you put *all* your money into this one account: wages, savings, everything. This reduces the interest you're charged on your mortgage because for a time you're essentially borrowing less, so you pay the loan off faster. Of course you have to take money out to pay bills, which lowers the total, but overall you're saving money.

The bad part is that these loans usually have a slighter higher interest rate than a standard loan. You need to decide if the benefits outweigh the extra interest. Banks sometimes will not give you a line of credit for the entire loan amount, in which case you may end up with both a line of credit and a smaller standard loan.

Line of credit loans can be dangerous. It's incredibly easy to spend wildly and never pay off the loan. Need a new car or holiday? Just draw on what you've paid off, great! Unfortunately this brings the loan back up to where you started. These loans only work for strict budgeters.

Mortgage insurance

There are two types of insurance, and it's very easy to be fooled. One insurance exists to protect the bank, the other to protect you.

Mortgage guarantee insurance is for the bank. If you have a small deposit, or are spending more to build/buy a house than the bank thinks it's worth, the bank may insist you pay mortgage guarantee insurance.

Mortgage protection insurance is for you. If you or your partner get seriously sick or permanently incapacitated, or if you are out of work for a long while, this insurance guarantees that the mortgage payments are still made. Some banks offer special deals. It's a convenience for their customers, and a way to make sure their investment is guaranteed. It's usually inexpensive and well worth it. Note that this insurance will only cover the mortgage payments. If you lose your job it won't cover food, utilities, car payments or other expenses. For full income protection you need to go to an insurance company, or get a life insurance policy with extras.

First Home Owner's Grant

You might qualify for a First Home Owner's Grant. Details vary from state to state, so ask your lender.

Miracle fast

Anyone can pay off a mortgage in only a few years. But there are catches (of course there are — there's no magic formula!). You've got to buy a very basic house with a very small mortgage. You've got to put literally every cent you have into it (less a tiny bit for luxuries so you don't feel you're in prison). But most people want *more* than just a basic house. And *more* than just a few luxuries. Not having a car saves you money, but you're also trapped unless there's really good public transport in your area.

Again, going somewhere in between may be the best answer: pay off the loan much faster than normal, but not so fast that every day is an extreme sacrifice. With good budgeting skills and the right mortgage, anyone can pay off an average 25–30 year mortgage in just eight to 12 years.

Now it's time to think about *creating* some wealth!

Increasing Wealth

You can't get rich by saving

You can spend almost nothing. You can budget for every conceivable expense. You can take advantage of every sale and special, voucher and deal. But no matter how hard you save, you can't get rich.

Saving is a great way to be efficient, but it's a terrible way to increase wealth. When you save, you're simply *not spending* from a limited income. If you make $30 000 a year, you've got $30 000 no matter how you spend or save. But saving won't bring in *extra* money.

And to get rich you need to have extra money. You can add to your income by taking a second job. Extra jobs add to your income, but they also add to your workload: you have to work harder to make more money. Eventually you'll run out of time and energy.

Who's the boss?

How can you make more money without spending too much time or energy? The answer is you can make your money work for you by using money to create more money. This is officially known as 'unearned income'. Bank interest is one form of unearned income. You allow the bank to use your money when you're not using it, and they pay you a very small fee for this service. You don't actually do any work and you get paid.

An investment is a better example. Say a computer nerd builds a new type of computer in his shed. He thinks this new machine will be a huge seller, but he doesn't have enough money to pay for testing and building, or for setting up a real business. You give him money and he'll do all the work. If he's successful you get your money back, plus a share of the ongoing profit. So the more computers he sells, the more money you continue to make. Unearned income.

In this example the nerd *was* successful, he was a real person who started a little company called Apple Computer. It's a true story that happened a long time ago to other people, so you'd need a time machine to go back and get in on that deal.

There are many big considerations when it comes to investment. How do you know a good deal when you see one? The computer nerd could be a no-talent hack who never leaves the shed, or he could have great computer skills, but no business expertise. Without a psychic glimpse into the future, it's difficult to know. A great-grandmother of ours had a chance to invest in American Telegraph & Telephone in the 1890s for a very small price. She thought telephones were very interesting, but not much use. 'Who would you call? Not many people have a telephone!' She decided against the investment, and missed out owning a part of AT&T at a cheap price. AT&T is now one of the largest telecommunications companies in the world. At the time, though, she had a point.

Good deal or not, there's a lot of risk. Another computer nerd could come up with a better computer, or your nerd could die and there'd be no one to run the business. He might get bought out and the whole direction of the business could change. The list of risks is endless. You also have to pay tax on all your unearned income. (But at least with unearned income the tax comes after the money. Your wage is taxed *before* you even see it. More on tax later.)

Unearned income is obviously a lot of work. That's why many people think it's too much trouble and are happy to plod along in their regular job, never investing. It *is* work, but the ratio of work-to-profit is much better than a regular job. You put in one unit of effort and get back many units of profit.

ThE SECrEt to making mONEy

There are more secrets to this money-making stuff. These are very important. They are the three basic, time-tested ways to make money (in no particular order):

1 Own a *business*
2 Invest in the *share market*
3 Invest in *real estate*

Really and truly, these are the main ways to increase your wealth. Anything else is either a variation, or something else that's not about creating money, like inheriting money or being born rich. Both are nice, but have nothing to do with creating new wealth.

Here we're going to cover each of the three basic ways of making money. You can choose how you increase your wealth, using one method or a combination of all three. Use them to create your own money machine.

But what if I win the lottery?

Great! You'll have a large pile of shrinking money. That's worth repeating: shrinking money. You need to invest even if you become rich. Otherwise the money gets spent without being replaced and it disappears very quickly. Yes, even if you win $10 million.

Money machine

To increase wealth you need to think differently. Instead of thinking that you'll come up with One Big Deal that will dump millions of dollars in your lap, think of building a machine that continuously creates small to medium amounts of money. We're not talking about a printing press, but a system. A collection of organised investments that once started, only needs a bit of maintenance to keep creating money. A money machine is far better than a job that forces you to put in one unit of effort for one unit (or less) of money.

Jewellery

Because jewellery is something you can touch, and because it's so expensive, many people think jewellery is a good investment — it's not.

If you like the sparkles and the feeling (and who doesn't?), and you've got extra money, then buy jewellery because it makes you feel good. Don't buy jewellery because you think you're converting cash to a solid investment.

Jewellery is difficult to resell at its value, unless you sell it privately (and then it's difficult to find a buyer). A valuation may show that a diamond and gold bracelet is worth $10 000, but try to sell it again to a jewellery store — you'll be lucky to get 10 to 30 per cent of the original value.

Design it

Everyone's money machine is different. You'll probably change the design and modify it as you and the machine grow. Create a balance of real estate, shares, and various small and medium businesses. Don't laugh, you can do it! It just takes time and persistence. And a plan.

If you're unsure about which direction to go, think about it in steps. Your immediate goal might be to work less (or at something more enjoyable), or maybe just to have extra money for luxuries and a happier lifestyle. So design a small money machine that will get you to that goal in six to 12 months. Think of alternative ideas in case the plan isn't working well after three or four months. Plan how to get to your next goal later, whether it's paying off all your debts, expanding your income greatly or planning for a wealthy retirement.

Build it

There's an old saying, 'plan your work and work your plan'. It means preparation is vital, but you must put the plan into action and keep it on course. Once you've learned and researched, you'll have to make your plan a reality by putting money into that first investment. Thinking about it, planning it and talking about it are all necessary. But the most important part is to break through that scary barrier of dream and hesitation, and do it. Go!

Turn it on

This type of machine runs as soon as you fit the first piece. It's an instant 'on'. But you'll have to maintain it, and observe the results. If the numbers aren't as expected, you might have to make a change and even rewrite your overall plan.

One of the most important points about investing is that you must be unemotional. Think like an engineer, not a dreamer. Don't close your eyes and wish or hope for good results. You're building a machine to make money, and you need to make all your decisions based on what works best. If the numbers don't work, keep trying until they do. Your whole purpose is to maximise your *return on investment* (ROI). You spend a little to make a lot. That includes time as well as money. All business investment, whether it's producing widgets or real estate, is about turning *some* money into a lot of money.

Now, let's start planning your money machine!

MiND your OWN business

Owning or being a part of a business is a great way to make money. Just look at all the businesses around you ... plumbers, electricians, newsagents, book shops, clothing shops, bakeries, butcher shops, supermarkets and more. Businesses that provide a service or a product. Small businesses, medium businesses, and even large corporations. Owning a business obviously works, or people wouldn't bother starting one.

Business is about constantly taking in money. Maybe not a million dollars a day, or even a year, but a steady profit. A business is about selling a chair for $90 and making a $10 profit. You have to sell a lot of chairs to get rich, but if you constantly sell chairs you have a steady, ongoing income.

A while back McDonald's restaurants spent US$900 million on advertising in one year. They don't do that every year, but they do spend a lot. You might be thinking that if you had $900 million you'd pack up and call it quits. But McDonald's knows it's all about maintaining a steady income, and part of keeping that income steady is to tell people about their product.

Most businesses like to make at least a 50–100 per cent profit on every item. At first this might sound like a rip-off for the consumer, but if you look at the whole chain it's simple compensation for service. It's also *gross* profit, meaning before expenses and tax.

Say your friend Dianne has a chair store. She buys the chairs ready-made from a master craftsman for $50 each. If Dianne sold the chairs for $50 you'd think she was an idiot, but you'd also think that she would at least *break even* or get back what she put in. Wrong! Dianne would actually *lose* money. Yes, she'd be getting what she paid for the chairs, but there are additional expenses. It probably cost Dianne some money to physically collect the chairs (petrol, time, effort). Then there's the rent she pays on her shop. Plus she employs one person — that's wages plus taxes and superannuation. She's also got to pay for electricity, insurance, telephone, postage, cleaning, advertising and bookkeeping. When that's all added up, Dianne has to charge a customer $90 so that she can make a $10 profit.

Chair from manufacturer	$50
Expenses	$30
Clear Profit (5.55%)	$10

You might think it would be cheaper and easier for customers to just buy direct from the manufacturer. But the manufacturer isn't equipped to sell to the public. The manufacturer doesn't have display space, salespeople, money or time for advertising and everything else that goes with it. If the manufacturer did have space, time and staff, the factory would be a retail shop like Dianne's and prices would go up.

Dianne also sells chair wax and chair magazines. The chair wax costs her $1 to buy from the manufacturer, Acme

Petrochemicals and Waxes. Dianne sells the wax for $12.50. There aren't really any other expenses, so it's very profitable. People are happy to pay $12.50 for a wax that 'beautifies and protects'. To customers, it feels like a fair price for the product. Dianne clears $11 on the wax, which equates to a profit of 92 per cent. It's easy to sell as an add-on and to people who already have chairs. If sales slump and the wax doesn't sell, Dianne can reduce the price to stimulate sales, or in an emergency she can throw it in as an added bonus to make customers feel like they're getting a great deal. Because it's so cheap and the staff are good salespeople, the wax is a big seller and profit-maker — or in the retail lingo, a *cash cow*.

The chair magazines are a different story. Everyone wants to buy the magazines to find the right new chair and to make sure they are using their existing chairs properly. Dianne doesn't make any money on magazines. The price is set by the publisher, and magazines cost a lot to produce. Dianne has to pay $4.95, and the suggested cover price is $5.25. But people won't come into the shop if Dianne doesn't stock the latest *Cushion & Seat* or *Sitting Monthly*. The magazines are a *loss leader*. Dianne must use the magazines to draw people into the store.

Buying yourself a job

Many people go into business so they can be their own boss. There are many satisfying benefits. When you make a decision it's quick and final; no arguments or time wasted convincing someone else that your ideas are good. You can plan and control your own workload and movements to your advantage. And of course, you get the profits.

But there are drawbacks. You *have* to make the

decisions, and they have to be good. If things go wrong, you're ultimately to blame. But the real problem with being your own boss is that it often means you're the whole business. If you're sick, you don't make money. And no matter how hard you work, you have limitations — there's only so much work you can handle, which means there's a very definite limit to how much money you can make. Often, the ratio of profit-to-effort is not very attractive: you have to work 12- and 14-hour days to make a normal living.

Ultimate goal

When you decide to work for yourself, it's important to remember that your ultimate goal is really to create a money-making machine, or unearned income. If you choose owning a business as the way to do this, keep that goal in mind. It may mean you start off with a one-person stand selling widgets, working long days and long nights. But your plan is to have a whole chain of stores in a few years and sit back counting your money.

The point is to get the business big enough to run smoothly without you, so it provides unearned income.

First step

So, you're thinking about getting into business. Everyone dreams of being their own boss. Sure, the hours are usually long and the work difficult, but there is a feeling of freedom and accomplishment. The effort is for you, not someone else.

There are a few different ways to get into business. If you're serious, you'll probably start small and eventually explore them all.

Network or multi-level marketing

We're going to explore network marketing a bit more than some other categories, because it can be dangerous and you should have all the facts before you make a decision about jumping into the business world this way. It can be a good way to *learn*, however, as long as you are armed with information and an exit plan.

Companies like Amway, Neways, Enjo, Postie Fashions and a hundred others, are network marketing companies. They have done all the research, created the procedures and set up the support materials. All you have to do is follow the instructions.

How it works

A network is a combined group. The Internet is a network of millions of individual computers that are all linked. ('Internet' is short for 'interconnected network'). All network marketing programs work on the same principle: you sell more than just a product; you sell the business itself. A hardware store sells screws, widgets and sprockets. But network marketing sells people. Not as in slavery, but as in other sales reps.

Here is an example: the network marketing company PyramidCo sells all-natural household cleaning products. Your friend Darren works part-time as a rep on top of his regular job. Darren says the products are cheap, environmentally friendly and do a great job. He saves heaps over the big commercial cleansers like Mr Acid and Germ Blaster. Darren convinces you that you like the products, too. 'How could you *not*? Do you want to throw away your money while you're destroying the earth with your harmful chemicals? You're not stupid.' So you buy some.

When it's time for more, Darren appears. Now he asks,

'How would you like to buy the products at a wholesale price?' Darren has shown you how inexpensive the products are anyway; if you buy them wholesale you'll be way ahead! You just have to become a PyramidCo sales rep, and then you'll pay wholesale for everything you buy. You sell some kits at retail price and keep the difference! Saving money and making money.

You jump at the chance. Darren lends you a few instruction tapes, but you have to buy some other tapes and manuals. You attend various training seminars, then you buy kits at wholesale and start selling.

You approach everyone and anyone. Friends, relatives, strangers on the street. Everyone you meet is an unexplored opportunity. You don't just try to get them to buy products, you try to turn them into reps, too, because you get a piece of profit from every rep below you, for *everything they order in the future*. And so does Darren, because he's above you. You've become a distributor.

If you can get ten people under you (or in the lingo, in your *downline*), you get money from the products they sell without having to do anything. And of course each of these people will try to get ten people, who will try to get ten people ... In two sets, or 'generations', you'll have 110 people below you! *That's* unearned income! Smell the money.

This is the network part of network marketing. People. But the other name for it is more accurate: multi-level marketing, or MLM. This is a better name because it is more accurate and descriptive. It's all about levels. You want to have as many people under you as possible to give you as much unearned income as possible. But remember, at the same time you're making everyone above you rich.

PyramidCo reps at the top, the founders and primary reps, are laughing! They're selling the product to all their reps to use at home, they're selling the product to all their reps to sell to others, and the reps are actively bringing more people on board to be a part of the whole cycle. Sure, PyramidCo has to reward all those below with commissions, but there's still heaps of profit. If you're dreaming of getting 110 people below you, there are probably already several thousand above.

As you can see, it's great to be at the top level, or not too far down. The more reps there are under you, the more money you make without actually working. That's why dishonest versions of this are called *pyramid schemes*. They're designed to funnel money to the top people. Usually the dishonest schemes are not about selling product at all; they're simply about sending money to others, like a complex chain letter. These types of schemes are not only dishonest, they are illegal.

The cold, hard truth

This might be a shock to some, but there isn't much difference between a dishonest, full-blown pyramid scheme and a legal, professional multi-level marketing program. The illegal pyramid schemes break the law, the MLMs do not. But the point of any MLM is for those at the top to get rich. There are some flaws in the plan if you are a long way down the chain.

Major flaw 1 — who is buying?

Reps are encouraged to sell only to other reps, and to spend their time creating new reps. To sell the product to 'outsiders' is a waste of time compared to creating more of a downline. That sounds fine, until you think about it: it really means that those in the top levels are simply selling the product to you and everyone below. The employees are the customers. Why is that? Because employees who are mesmerised by the sales pitch and are blindly loyal will continue to buy the product even when they are having trouble selling it. It's a little like tobacco companies and addicted customers. But if only employees are buying, who's buying from those stuck at the bottom?

Major flaw 2 — limits

No matter how good or bad your product or pitch, some people are never going to buy or become involved. It's the same with any product or service. Some people can be convinced, some can't.

After a time, many of those involved in MLM, including reps in your precious downline, will lose interest and stop buying or drop out completely. It's true of anything, not just MLM. Most humans peak and move on after a time.

Your infinite downline is actually very finite. You'll hit every person you know and everyone they know, probably offending and losing friends in the process. If you make a list of 20 people you could hit, and ask them each to make a list of 20 people they know, that's 400 potentials. Part of that 400, though, is a common pool of people that you all know. Maybe that reduces the number of potentials down to say 250. And because it's impossible to convince everyone of anything, out of all those potentials you'll end up with somewhere around 10–20 per cent, or about 50 people. (Direct mail is about a 1–3 per cent response rate.) Fifty is a very, very high number — maybe too high. It's probably accurate to say 25. How many of those 25 will go the distance? And those 25 will be selling to some of the same people. Market saturation will occur quickly.

Major flaw 3 — price

The retail price of the products is advertised as cheap or competitive. In reality, it's not much different from regular or sale prices. Many of the products have a fair unit price, but they have to be purchased in extreme bulk. Bulk that couldn't be used in a lifetime.

How to make MLM work

Some people have actually made heaps of money in legal MLM companies. They buy cars, they travel, they get written up in the company magazines. It is not impossible, but it requires a few key elements: great sales ability, luck, hard work, and being near the top level early in the game. Most of the big MLMs are about 20 years old; one is over 40 years old. Even with people dropping out, that's a lot of people who will be above you.

Sales training is provided, and you're taught well-proven, field-tested selling methods. In fact, there are even scripts to learn to help you sell. But you still have to have confidence, and those with natural or learned sales ability go much further than those who stumble through the pitch like robots. In the end, it's up to you.

Will MLM be your professional business life? Based on the simple facts, MLM could be a good way to learn. Tell yourself you'll do it for four to six months. If you're making a profit, stay in. But make sure you don't get addicted and end up buying products without selling them, or that you take in a lot of money but find that after expenses you have actually lost a lot of money.

Be prepared to pester everyone you know and meet. Because at the bottom, when you're just starting out, you'll have to work hard not to lose money. Remember, you've got to buy the products before you sell them, whereas other types of companies supply the product to you and pay you a commission on units sold. If you can swing it, get orders from your downline *before* you buy from your upline. This way, you're not out of pocket if sales are down.

Things to look for

Choose an honest, successful company that has a history and a good reputation. Is that possible? We'll assume it is, at least as far as choosing a company that doesn't ask you to pay a $5000 deposit to start up. You'll have to buy kits and probably spend a little on some training materials, but don't spend thousands and start flying to $500 company seminars on the other side of the country.

If it is a new company, is it successful? Is it a potentially good market? Research carefully. You can get some basic information and reports on the web simply by doing a few searches. Buy a consumer affairs magazine such as Choice, or check with Consumer and Business Affairs in your state (in the White Pages under 'Government'). Ask people you know if they've bought from the company, or try to buy something yourself and listen first-hand to what a rep has to say.

Bad (and sadly, sometimes good) companies alike will try to pressure you into the program because all they can see are profits below them. *Do not* be pressured. If it all seems too good to be true, then it probably *is* too good to be true. Remember, the first core secret to getting rich: There is no magic!

The whole point of MLM is that you are trained in a system that works. That way, you only have to follow instructions and sell the product. And if you're lucky, live off the people below you.

Major MLMs

Most network marketing organisations offer information on their websites, but to become a rep you need to be sponsored by an existing rep (your *upline*). If you really want to join a company, check out community bulletin boards in front of the supermarket or library, and check their websites. You may even know someone in MLM already. (You probably do, at least someone who has experimented.)

Amway International
www.a2k.com.au
Products: Huge range of health and beauty products, cleansers and more. All are either natural or not harmful to the environment.
History: Founded in 1959 by Richard DeVos and Jay Van Andel. Operates in 80 countries and territories; 3.5 million reps (or 'independent business owners' in the Amway lingo), 115 000 of these in Australia.

Neways International
www.neways.com.au
Email: info@neways.com.au
Products: Huge range of health and beauty products, cleansers and more. All are either natural or not harmful to the environment.
History: Founded in 1987 by Tom and Dee Mower. Australian office opened in 1989. Operates in 38 countries.
Mission statement/promotional slogan: *Bridging the gap between science and human needs.*

Enjo International
www.enjo.com.au
1800 648 334 (for nearest consultant)
Products: Fibre-based cleaning supplies that only need water to clean (reduces the need for chemical cleansers).
History: Founded in 1993 by Barb de Corti in Western Australia. 2000 Australian reps.
Mission statement/promotional slogan: *Clean the world.*

Postie Fashions
www.postie.com.au
Products: Clothing to suit every taste, in sizes 6–28.

History: Founded in 1987 by Stephen and Ann
Wilson. Australian company.
Mission statement/promotional slogan: *Open your door
to a new way of fashion shopping ... open your door to
Postie.*

Herbalife
www.herbalife.com/au
Products: Weight loss products.
History: Founded in 1980 by Mark Hughes. Operates
in 58 countries with one million reps.
Mission statement/promotional slogan: *Here we grow!*

Buying into a business

Becoming a silent partner

If you don't want to work hard but still want to be in
business, you can invest in an existing business as a silent
partner. This involves giving money to an established
business in return for a part of the profits. It's a private
version of buying shares. In fact, when you sign a contract
and hand over your money, you might actually be getting
non-public shares in the business in return. The details vary
from deal to deal, but the principle is the same: you give
money, the business gives money back.

You don't have any say in management or any other
part of the business, but you also don't have any headaches.
A problem with this type of opportunity, however, is that it
can be very risky. Why does the business need a partner? A
partner that brings no skills or active participation to the
business is a drain on profits. If the business needs a partner
to allow it to expand, then that's a positive reason (though
still a risk). If it needs a partner because business is bad, you
could be throwing away money.

The deal itself can be tricky too. The best deal will give
you as much profit as possible for as little risk as possible, at

a low cost. If the deal gives you shares, are you responsible for debt beyond your investment? Can you be sued by people who think the business owes them money?

A silent partner deal can be profitable, but it can be limiting. It's the sort of investment that on the whole, as a category of investments, is mediocre. But individually, in terms of any specific deal you may make, it can be either terrible or terrific.

There is no silent partner hotline to call to find out about opportunities, but you can often find deals by word-of-mouth. Keep your ears open. Often a friend's cousin's mate's acquaintance has a business and is looking for outside investment. The business section of many newspapers will have large segments on buying businesses and franchises. Often accountants and solicitors who specialise in business will have advertisements. They might have a client looking for an investor. Call them and ask!

Buying an established business

If you're ready to go to work for yourself but don't have the experience and resources to start a business from scratch, you can buy one off the shelf. You can either buy into a franchise, or buy a private business. You can work in the business, or you can hire a manager. Even if you start off doing it yourself, never forget your ultimate goal: to sit back and let the business make money for you.

Franchises

A franchise is an individual link in a chain of stores. Each store is independently owned, but all the stores are part of the same company. Examples of franchises include McDonald's, Mitre 10, The Cheesecake Shop, Subway, Ultra Tune and Jim's Mowing.

Details vary from company to company, but the

advantages are the same: someone else has built the business. You just invest some money and follow the directions. It's like network marketing in that respect. The testing is done, the procedures are in place and it works. You don't even have to advertise, you simply contribute money to the national advertising campaign.

How it works

You love widgets and think there's a big market in your area. You approach the Widgets-R-Us chain about buying a franchise. The price is $75 000, plus expenses to set up a shop. The company provides all training and advertising. You pay a monthly and/or yearly franchise fee as a percentage of profits that covers advertising, equipment, procedures, and selling under the most respected name in widgets.

You take savings and probably a loan from the bank, and you buy into the franchise. You follow the company procedures and pay your franchise fees. Either the business is the right size from the start to allow you to sit back and let someone else manage it, or you work towards this goal. It's that simple. (Plus the hard work, of course!)

Some companies have strict procedures, like McDonald's. They spend a lot of money on operations and advertising, and they have a lot riding on the gamble that a new franchisee will do the job right, without hurting the McDonald's trade name. So they limit the risk as much as possible by training you thoroughly and restricting your power. Walk into any McDonald's anywhere in the world and you could be, well, anywhere in the world. Details vary, but the equipment and layout is about the same in any store. The menu is the same, except for trial specials and local popular products. Some outlets have carefully researched individual themes to make them seem funky and unique.

You may be little more than an employee, even when you own the store! But the procedures are so tried-and-true you don't have to think, just act.

Other companies provide the base, but expect you to make it all work. There may be restrictions, but for the most part you can manage and operate on your own while still enjoying the benefits of a franchise.

What to look for

Some smaller franchises are really more interested in taking franchise money than whether you'll be a successful on-going business. That's short-sighted, because it's a bit like multi-level marketing. If the market is over-saturated, everyone is hurt. Good franchisers will help you to be successful, because you're helping them to be successful.

Be careful to choose a business that is prospering and has a good reputation, both in the business world and with customers. Have you shopped there yourself? Choose businesses you like and are excited about. Having a job you like will make your life easier, and you're more likely to perform better (and make more money) if you are enthusiastic about the business and products.

Established private business

You love widgets. You can't think of anything more satisfying than selling those steely gizmos. But instead of buying into a franchise, you'd rather have the business (and widgets) all to yourself. Rather than being a silent partner, you want to be more hands-on, so that you get to touch and feel all the widgets. Don't like the 1-ply stamped model? Don't sell it! (Unless it's hugely popular.) You make the decisions. You control the operation.

Buying a private business will mean more work, but because it is an ongoing business with a history and existing customers, you have structure and guidelines to follow. This part is like a franchise, in the sense that the business is set up and running. But it is also more work than a franchise, because all the future decisions are yours to make. You'll be on your own, without corporate support or experience. However, it is much less work than establishing a business from scratch.

How it works

When you buy an existing business you're buying what you can see — the premises, the inventory and the equipment. You buy the touchable parts of the business. But you also get the business name, which has years of good history associated with it (or years of bad!) Think of the company BHP and you probably think, 'years of steel, solid, a backbone of the Australian economy'. Think of Microsoft and you probably think 'huge and powerful', but for some people that can mean 'big, scary, and maybe a little unapproachable'.

Once you've found a business that looks good, you have to make sure it *is* good. Why are the current owners selling? They might say it's because they're changing their lifestyle and moving, or maybe they're tired of widgets (how could you be tired of widgets?), or going into another business, or any other innocent reason. The list is endless. But find out if there's a more financially dangerous reason, like widget sales have dropped, or a major widget manufacturer is on the edge of financial disaster. Sometimes it's a matter of asking straight out: 'Is there anything hidden that will hinder me from running the business successfully?' Honest people will tell you.

The business's financial books ('the books') should tell the real story. The owners might say they're very optimistic about sales even though business has been slow recently.

Great sales talk, but what do the books say? The books never lie. Well, sometimes they do. People have been doctoring, or 'cooking', the books for centuries. That's where a good accountant comes in.

If you're serious about a particular business, it's worth hiring an accountant to check the books. Think of it like getting a building inspector to check out a house, or having a vehicle inspector look at a used car. If you're not sure, always bring in an expert. Don't be embarrassed if you can't make heads or tails of the figures. That's what accountants do. It may cost a few hundred dollars, but in the long term it's money well spent. Some accountants specialise in business valuations and investigations, or offer consulting and tax advice.

Business brokers

When you want to buy a house, you go to a real estate agent. When you want to buy a business, you go to a business broker. They don't sell commercial properties; they sell businesses. The building, the name, the inventory, the equipment, the whole business. You can find a local business broker in the business section of the newspaper, and in the Yellow Pages.

If figures and accounting are not your area of expertise, then buying an established business is definitely a lot easier than building one.

What to look for

Cash flow The business should have a healthy cash flow. It should be making money, or there isn't any point in buying it. This has to be actual money flow in to the business, not potential or intangible assets.

Growth Look back through the records for two or three years. The business should have grown, even a little, each year. Businesses that don't grow actually shrink. Without taking a huge economics detour here, it's like when Dianne was going to buy her chairs for $50 and sell them for $50. Because of expenses, Dianne was going to lose money, not break even. The same goes for a business that hasn't grown, due to inflation, wage rises, the cost of turning raw materials into products rises, and so on.

For example, say the target business sold 10 000 widgets three years ago, at a net profit (after expenses and tax) of 10 per cent. But costs have risen over the past couple of years, and by the time you look at the business it's still only selling 10 000 widgets a year and net profit is now 8 per cent. If you take over, you can either raise the price or try to sell more. A price rise might scare off some customers and lower sales, yet it may be more difficult to sell extra widgets at the regular price. The business would be healthier if it gained more and more customers over the years, or if present customers increased orders.

Existing customers Is there a healthy base of regulars and account customers? Most business comes from existing customers. It's easier to sell to regulars than it is to get new customers.

Equipment Any equipment needed in the business probably comes along as part of the deal. Does it function well? When will you need to update to a newer, bigger (or smaller) model? Have all tax depreciation benefits been taken? Will you be forced to buy all new fromulators at a huge expense? Is the equipment owned outright, or are there any leases, contracts or debts? Answering yes to any of these negative-sounding questions is not necessarily bad; you just have to plan and react accordingly. Accountants can help.

The building Does the building come as part of the deal, or is it leased? If it is leased, what are the terms? You don't want to buy a business that depends on its existing premises, only to find that the lease will expire in two months and you'll be hard pressed to find a new location and suitable building.

Inventory The inventory is the product you sell or the raw materials for making the product. Does it come with the business? If not, how much extra will it be?

Employees Are there key people whose expertise can't easily be duplicated? In other words, would you be dependent on one or two people, and will they come with the deal or will you have to replace them? If your new operation does depend on key people, make sure you have plans to treat them well and train backups or replacements.

What to avoid

Debt Does the business owe any money? It could be debts to suppliers (*creditors*), loans, or taxes and penalties.

Legal Are there any lawsuits pending against the company, or against customers? How will these affect you financially?

What's missing Has the owner taken anything out of the business? Sometimes dishonest business owners will strip the company of cash, hide it as best they can, then hit the road. They might also have cash arrangements with certain employees in an attempt to avoid various employer and employee taxes. Advice to owners: Don't! You're cheating your fellow citizens by not meeting your tax responsibility, and it's a sure way to attract heavy penalties. The Tax Office has a way of finding out and they don't have a sense of humour. Being dishonest can be quite dangerous, but it's especially dangerous when it involves tax.

Obviously, there are plenty of nitty gritty details that

are important. We can't list them all, but this is where experts become invaluable. Free services are useful for general information, but you will probably end up paying a professional, like an accountant and/or business broker.

Business Entry Point

The Business Entry Point is a government website for people starting or running a business. The site has plenty of information on everything you need to know (structure, employees, accounting, tax, sales, operations, management and more). It's a federal site with links to each state. A great resource — go to www.business.gov.au.

Starting a business from scratch

Starting a business from scratch is a huge undertaking, even for the experienced. We'll cover all the major points and make sure you have solid information. If you are serious about it, though, you should get specific professional advice. It would be best if you could gain experience and training in a smaller venture first.

A new business is a lot of work, but when all the pieces come together it can be very rewarding; both in fulfilment and profits.

In the beginning

It's important to plan carefully. Most new businesses fail in the first few years, often because the owners and managers aren't prepared. If you don't have a passion for a product or service and just want to be in business, it might be better to buy an existing business or franchise. You've got to make a business work, and that means dedication.

Good reasons to start your own business

1   You have a new product or service
2   You have a new way of doing business
3   There's a need for a certain type of business in a particular area
4   You have a particular profitable talent
5   You understand money-making so well that you have a Midas touch, and it would be almost a crime not to put your talents to use
6   An amazing opportunity pops up (or you make one).

If your reasons equal good business, then you need to see if your business idea will work in your area and in your particular circumstances.

Market

Is there a definite, measurable group of people who will buy your product/service? If so, what will they pay, and is that enough to make the business worthwhile? Will it grow or shrink?

No one can answer these questions completely and positively, but you will have to get some accurate numbers as a general indicator. Not only will the information be very useful to you, but your bank and any partners or investors will insist on it. It relates directly to how much money you'll make. Professional marketing companies and the Australian Bureau of Statistics can help; visit their website at www.abs.gov.au.

Cost and profit

How much will you have left after expenses? When estimating profit, don't be emotional or hopeful, be brutally honest. Use numbers and established facts.

For example, you plan to sell widgets and you know from personal shopping experience that most widgets sell for about $25–30. You want to boost sales and really compete with the other widget stores, so you decide to sell them for only $18. This is following your heart and not your head.

Start at the very beginning and work through the numbers: a widget manufacturer will sell you widgets for $10 each. That's a fixed cost you can't control (though you might pay less later if you order a huge quantity). The manufacturer's *recommended retail price* (RRP) is $25. Even though you 'just know' the usual price for a widget, you do research and find that competitors are selling widgets for between $20 and $29. You could stick with the RRP from the manufacturer, or you could add all the prices together and get an average, and then make adjustments up or down:

$$\$20 + \$25 + \$29 = \$74 \div 3 = RRP \ \$24.66$$

To boost initial sales and be competitive, you decide on a retail price of $22.50. You've now got your cost and RRP. $22.50 − $10.00 = $12.50 gross profit (before expenses and tax).

$12.50 sounds good, but can the business work at this price? You also have to consider your other expenses.

ONGOING (monthly)

Shop rent/mortgage	$500.00
Insurance	50.00
Telephone	100.00
Electricity	350.00
Maintenance	50.00
Wages	700.00
Office (stationery, postage)	50.00
Advertising	500.00
and more	
Estimated total	$2300.00

With expenses of $2300 a month, you would need to sell 184 widgets every month just to break even ($2300 ÷ $12.50 = 184). Then any units beyond 184 would equal pure profit ($22.50 − $10 Cost = $12.50 Profit).

And don't forget the original start-up costs. You would probably need a loan to buy equipment and set up the shop. This will have to be paid off. For this example, assume another expense of bank loan (loan plus interest) of $800 per month for three years. This means you'll have to sell a minimum of 240 widgets a month to break even.

You've got your costs worked out; can the market in your area sustain say, 250–300 widgets a month?

(Note that the above example is simplified and does not include GST or any tax issues.)

Competition

Maybe the potential market is good, but there are already widget shops in the area. Should you give up before you start? No, don't panic. Competition can be healthy. As long as the market is large, more than one widget shop can actually increase sales for both shops.

Look at the oil companies with competing petrol stations across the street from each other. They know that they'll both catch some of the traffic. They also know that, thanks to advertising, some motorists have been brainwashed into brand loyalty and will go out of their way to shop with one or the other. (Petrol is a lot like the rice example mentioned earlier: if it's clean and made to industry standards, then it's good stuff no matter what the brand.)

Brand loyalty, or 'false competition' as we prefer to call it, persuades people to buy, sometimes to impress their friends and neighbours. If you look at the labels on nappies you'll find that several of the brands are actually made by the same company. But young parents swear by one brand over another. Many moisturising creams are made the same way, with negligible difference in formulas, yet some sell for $80 a tube and others for only $2. People who like to maintain a certain image are happy to spend more to show off, and those with smaller budgets get along with the less expensive stuff. Together, they are driving the economy!

But competition is only good if the market is big enough. Three furniture stores in an outback town with 100 people would be three furniture stores too many.

Not working

If you find the numbers don't quite work for your business, don't panic. Thomas Edison conducted literally thousands of experiments to make his light globe work. He was eventually successful, but he could have given up. You might have to wait a while for the right conditions, or change a key part of the business (location, products, market). If you can't make it work on paper and professional advice doesn't help, you can wait until you see another opportunity. Notice we said 'see'. Opportunities rarely announce themselves and say 'Hello, I'm a perfect opportunity that requires no thought or effort!' More likely, opportunities will be hiding in plain sight right in front of you. It's up to you to recognise them and act.

Solid as a rock

There are two secrets of running a profitable business: start with a solid foundation, and keep ongoing costs (*overheads*) to a minimum. Too many businesses struggle to keep their doors open, all the while working too hard for a small profit that's eaten up by problems and inefficiency.

If you were going to open, say, a restaurant, it would make sense to find the best chef you could and pay him or her a bit more than the standard. Then find someone almost as good as an assistant chef. (The assistant could take over in an emergency, like when the head chef storms out because you said his vichyssoise needed salt.) Then do the same for the manager and assistant manager. Target a certain slice of the public and create a suitable menu. Put your restaurant in an attractive, convenient location and then just watch the money roll in!

The point is to build a solid machine. The key pieces in this example are happy, professional people, great food and great location. Of course, you'd also have to do some research, planning, and handle the odd emergency, but you would be prepared.

Employees

Employees are expensive by nature. Aside from wages, there are superannuation payments, taxes and paperwork, all tightly controlled by the government. There are strictly enforced laws that stop businesses from paying employees in cash, or taking advantage of employees by forcing them to work long hours for little pay. (That said, it still happens.) Penalties include heavy fines and court headaches.

Employees are a responsibility. The people who work for you expect to be treated fairly and honestly, and they expect a pay packet every week, fortnight or month. You are probably an employee now, or have been in the past. You know what you expect from the business you work for: a fair wage for a fair day's work, safe work environment and conditions. As an employer, you'll have to provide the same.

Some small businesses try to hire people as contractors, thus avoiding payroll costs like tax and superannuation. The

Tax Office is aware of this trick and has introduced severe restrictions. For example, if you hire a contractor to work in your business, they are considered an employee if you provide 80 per cent of their work.

Go over the numbers with an accountant to figure out how many workers you can afford, and what gains they'll bring to the business. Then you'll have to make the effort and set up employees properly. This means taxes, payments and paperwork.

We believe in finding skilled people and treating them well. It's not eating into profits to maintain the tools that create the profits.

Economy of scale

This doesn't mean a bathroom scale that's on sale; it simply means making the numbers work. If Dianne's chair store is very busy and she and her staff of one can't keep up, she's going to have to think about hiring one more rep or she'll lose customers. People don't want to wait 20 minutes while Dianne and her sales clerk sell chairs to other people.

So Dianne does the numbers. She'll pay a standard casual wage of $15 per hour. That's $570 a week, plus superannuation and other costs. In the end it may cost Dianne about $695 for another employee.

To cover the extra cost, Dianne will now have to sell about 25 more chairs. But with the extra staff, Dianne can probably sell 35 more chairs, so it would definitely be worth hiring an extra staff member.

If Dianne hired two more people she couldn't sell enough chairs to pay the extra staff. If there's still a big demand for chairs though, Dianne could think about opening another store in another location ...

A business plan

You've done your research, and your business idea looks good. Now you've got to form a plan and put it into action. This applies to buying an existing business or starting from scratch. Whether you've got plenty of *capital* (starting money) to work with, or you need a loan and/or investors, you'll definitely need a business plan. A plan prepares you for future problems and helps you grow strong and steady.

A plan will also show the banks, investors and advisors that you know what you're doing and that you've made a blueprint for success. There are standard formats and even templates available for business plans. Keep in mind the major points outlined below.

A plan must be complete, easy to understand and well thought out. It must be changeable, and allow for things to happen in the future. Being unprepared for something positive, like a huge boost in sales overnight, is as dangerous as being unprepared for disaster. You can't have all the answers, and you can't plan for every contingency, but you can be prepared to make up a new plan when a situation changes quickly and drastically.

Your plan has to be based on real-life facts and practices, not on what you'd like to believe. It's got to be unemotional. If the numbers don't add up, be honest. Look for another way, or make adjustments. In the end, it's got to be logical and workable. If it's not, you can fool yourself into financial ruin.

A business plan should describe:

1   The business and its products/services
2   What makes it a good business (why will it make money)
3   Marketing — research and future plans
4   Management — how the business will run

In short, you've got to answer every potential question to prove that you have the knowledge and expertise to risk time and money on the idea.

Business structure

Your business needs a legal form so that it exists either in addition to your personal finances or separately. There are three basic business forms, and each has advantages and disadvantages. There is no 'correct' choice, only the choice that is right for you. You may start with one and change later. For legal and tax advice, speak with an accountant and/or a solicitor.

Sole trader

The simplest business form is that of a sole trader. This means you do business as an individual. Your business income is added to any personal income, and you are taxed as a regular person at the appropriate rate.

Because you are in business, it's likely (hopefully!) that you will make much more money than you would as an employee in a regular job. So your tax rate will be higher, too.

Sole traders are personally responsible for their business's legal troubles, such as debt and liability. If your business is sued you may have to sell your house to cover damages.

A sole trader business is simple, inexpensive to set up, and easy to run. But you'll eventually be paying a high tax rate, and you can be personally financially responsible for business debts and legal costs.

To start up as a sole trader, you need to register a business name, get an ABN (contact the Tax Office) and open a separate bank account just for the business.

Partnership

Most people recognise the strength of having a partner. That's why many people get married. Unfortunately, many also get divorced. When choosing a business partner it's important to choose someone who complements you. Not as in 'nice shirt, Ralph', but someone whose strengths make up for your weaknesses. An example of a great combination is an artist and a salesperson. The artist can be creative but may know little about running a business; the salesperson can sell but may know little about being creative. Together they are stronger than the sum of their parts. This is not to say that two artists or two salespeople can't team up. Just make sure you have real business reasons to be partners.

A business partnership is much like someone operating as a sole trader, except that there are two or more of you. The tax and operations issues are almost the same as for a sole trader; the only difference is that business income is split between all the partners for tax purposes. If you've set up the business so that you are equal partners (50 per cent each), then tax and legal liability are split 50/50. If you're 60/40 partners, it's split 60/40. Your financial and legal obligations are split whatever way your partnership is set up. The only inequality occurs if one partner does something stupid — then you're both legally responsible.

You will need a partnership agreement, or a legal document stating the duties, responsibilities and rewards of the partnership. The agreement can be very short, simple and straightforward, as long as it meets legal requirements. A solicitor can set up a proper agreement, but any agreement must cover:

1   Who the partners are (names and addresses)
2   What type of business you will conduct (can often be very open)
3   The partners' rights and responsibilities

4   What will happen in certain circumstances (if partners dissolve, owe money etc.)

A partnership only lasts for the life of the partners, much as sole trading does. When the people who are the business stop doing business or die, there is no more business.

Business name

To register a business name, go to the Office of Business and Consumer Affairs in your state. It costs about $150 for two years. You usually have to provide between three and six name choices, in order of preference. Complex rules apply to prevent similar businesses from having similar names. Often you are encouraged to do a name search on the site first, then make a list. Once it is registered, you are given a certificate that you must display plainly in your main place of business.

You don't have to register a name if you'll be trading as a sole trader under your own name. For example, if Ralph chose to be a sole trader he could call his shop Ralph Blodget. He couldn't call it Ralph Blodget Widgets, though, without registering the name.

Get your name registered before having stationery printed, websites created, etc. Even when it's 'practically guaranteed', the name could be changed before it's finalised. Don't risk it.

Proprietary limited companies

Proprietary limited (Pty Ltd) companies are very 'business-like' forms of business. It means that your company exists separately as its own legal entity. The company itself can own property and equipment, it can buy and sell, and it can be sued. For example, the company photocopier is owned by the company, not you, even though it's your business.

Liability is limited to the company, a 'living' entity that has assets. You are not personally responsible for financial and legal damage. In theory. You can still be sued under some circumstances, but there's much, much more protection when you operate as a proprietary limited company.

All proprietary limited companies pay one tax rate — 30 per cent. If you are small and just starting out, this can seem high. As a sole trader the amount of income your business brings in might put you well below the 30 per cent rate. But as you grow, the income might put you well above that, into the 48.5 per cent rate.

Proprietary limited companies are expensive and complex to set up. There's an enormous amount of paperwork involved to start up, and it continues for the life of the company. Though it is technically possible to start up a proprietary limited company yourself, we don't recommend it. The money saved is minor compared to the effort involved.

A compromise between doing everything yourself and having a lawyer do it would be to have your lawyer buy a shelf company. This is a proprietary limited company that has been set up but either has never actually done business, or has wound up business and is in storage, or 'on the shelf'. Instead of the $1500-$2000 approximate cost to set up a company from scratch, you might pay $600–800 for a shelf company. You will most likely want to change the name, and you will have to change the directors. There are fees and paperwork, but it can still be cheaper and easier than starting from scratch. Be careful that the shelf company you choose doesn't have any outstanding debts or liabilities.

A proprietary limited company requires a minimum of one director, one shareholder and one company secretary. One person can be all three. Proprietary limited companies must follow corporations law (policed by the Australian

Securities and Investments Commission). A company constitution must be drawn up (and meet strict rules). This is like a partnership agreement.

Maintaining the machine

When you start a business you have to tell people — you need the customers. Shout it from the treetops! But as you go along you'll also have to continuously remind people that you've got products they want. What are we talking about? Advertising. Which is not the same thing as marketing.

Marketing could also be called selling. It's everything you've got to do to sell the product. It's a combination of product (what you sell), price (how much customers pay), distribution (how you get the product to the customers), and advertising (telling people about your product and the business itself).

You can hire professional advertising agencies and marketing companies, you can do it all yourself, or you can use a combination. Professionals have a lot of resources and experience, but they also sell a service.

All too often people buy hours and hours of advertising time on the radio or TV at great cost, but they get poor results. The advertising and marketing companies are selling lots of airtime, but the businesses don't get the sales unless the right audience is targeted. With tighter budgets, businesses are forced to aim for a better response (*pull*, in the lingo) to make spending the money worth their while. They have to target specific audiences and spend less money. Instead of making an expensive TV ad that reaches everybody, it can be better to focus on a small group. Newspapers or radio are good, but they are still broadcast mediums, and are wide-reaching. Specific publications aimed at a specific group are more effective. Like the *Widget*

Hobby News. Why waste $15 000 on a TV ad that won't interest most of the audience, when you can spend $300 on a print ad aimed only at people definitely interested in your product?

If you tackle advertising yourself, even a little, learn what works best. Marketing is quite complex, but you can look at examples all around you, especially things you buy. What made you buy that car/stereo/dishwasher? Was it an ad in a magazine, word-of-mouth, TV, a flyer? How did the product get to you? Were you in a shop and it caught your eye? What was the packaging like? Were you disappointed when you opened the box, or was it exciting, confirming that you made a wise choice?

We now buy our laser printer toner from a small, local business run by a semi-retired gentleman. Why? He sold us on his business and has kept us coming back. It started with a flyer we received in the mail. The flyer played up discounts, but in a solid, professional way, nothing low quality. We inquired about our toner because it's expensive and unusual. He knew technical details about it, which many don't, so immediately we had enough confidence to give him a try. He personally delivered the toner, accompanied by a few mints, in a little bag with his card. He also picked up the spent cartridge for recycling (realistically, he does get a small amount of money for this). Later in the year he sent us a Christmas card. Now when we run out of toner, who do we think of? A big shop in the city? A discount mail order company? Or the local we consider one of the family, with great service and prices? We recommended him to clients, too.

Build a better mousetrap

Maybe you don't want to run a full-blown business, but have a searing hot idea for a great little product. You just know it'll be a huge success and will make you rich. But how do you turn an idea into cash?

It's hard work. Rarely can you just sell an idea outright and walk away with heaps of cash. Ideas are everywhere. Anyone can have a good idea, but to turn one into an actual saleable product (or service) takes knowledge, commitment and perspiration (and some luck too). There are a few questions you need to ask yourself:

Does it already exist? You'd be surprised at how many times the toaster has been 'invented'. (Two people invented the telephone and ship's chronometer, but only one in each circumstance was able to get a patent.)

Is it something people actually want, or just something you want? And notice that we said 'want', not 'need'. People buy stuff they like, whether they need it or not. There's no point in making 100 000 flanglehoozies if no one wants them. You might sell ten, but selling to your immediate family doesn't count.

Can it be protected? Once you release it, will others copy it? Patents, trademarks and copyright can sometimes offer limited protection, but if it's cheap and easy to make, others will make it regardless of the law. The Tamagotchi virtual pet was little more than a sophisticated digital watch. Once the craze began, competitor's copies appeared under various names. The market was over-saturated and eventually the demand dried up. Still, both the creators and competitors made a lot of money. For a short while, anyway!

So your idea passes the above tests. What next? One of the major differences between success and failure is planning. Most people might build a danglehopper in their back shed and sell a few at markets, shows and swap meets. But the successful entrepreneur will make a plan, research, find smart people and create a blueprint for success. Also, if it's appropriate, think big: a silent partner, selling shares, raising capital, a worldwide marketing plan.

That's where many fail. They realise they don't have the expertise, so they keep it small. Those more likely to succeed will find others who are more business-savvy and get the help they need. Often accountants and solicitors can help organise capital, or seed money. Share the profit if necessary. One hundred per cent profit of $10 000 that you make by yourself is not as good as 25 per cent of $10 million. For those of you reaching for your calculator, trust us, the latter works out slightly more.

The difference is this: thinking small turns into extra income; thinking professionally turns into unearned income. Think professionally and you'll see your money machine humming along.

Trademarks, service marks and other marks

If establishing a brand (brand recognition) is important to you, then you can have your logo trademarked. Detailed information is available from the IP Australia (intellectual property) website (www.ipaustralia.gov.au). You pay a fee of about $500 and submit a sample of your company logo or item model logo. Once it is established that there are no other similar marks, you are granted the right to display the registered trademark symbol (®) and to protect your mark. Any competitors who trade on your mark or something that is too similar can be forced to stop, and pay a fine and damages. This can be a complex issue; seek advice from both the IP website and a solicitor.

Note that if you cheat and add the ® to unregistered work you can be penalised, which can include fines and a registration ban.

A service mark is like a trademark, but applies to non-tangible products, such as a service.

A patent gives the inventor of a new and original product the right to 'exclude all others' from making and selling the product, for a limited time. This only applies to new inventions.

A registered design is a sort of patent on a specific product styling (though this can include construction methods). 'Styling' means the visual design.

GST

The goods and services tax is a tax on consumer goods, services, and just about everything you can build or buy. Most modern countries have a similar tax, though it goes by various names: VAT (Value Added Tax) in the UK and Europe, and just plain sales tax in the US. It ranges throughout the world on average from 5 to 15 per cent. In Australia it's 10 per cent.

Before the GST, there was a 22 per cent wholesale sales tax which was added to the wholesale (supplier) price.

Now, GST is added to the final retail price of a product or service. If you were selling a widget for $10 you would have to add 10 per cent GST, for a final consumer price of $11. You would collect the GST from the customer and pass it on to the Tax Office.

Here's a little-known fact: Businesses don't pay GST. They pay it temporarily, but they eventually get it back. Only retail consumers pay GST. It works like this:

An ore producer, OreCo, smelts titanium ore. They sell it to a widget manufacturer, RaWidgets, for $1.10 per kilo (that's $1.00 + $0.10 GST). OreCo sends the $0.10 to the Tax Office.

RaWidgets turns the metal into widgets and sells them

to you, Widgets R Us, for $2.20 ($2.00 + $0.20 GST). Because they have already paid $0.10 GST to OreCo, RaWidgets keeps $0.10 and passes on the other $0.10 to the Tax Office.

When you sell a widget to the public for $11, you keep $0.20 to cover the GST you paid for the widget, and pass on $0.80 to the Tax Office.

Each business has collected and passed on GST to the Tax Office, minus whatever GST they had paid in the chain. Only the end-consumer has actually paid GST.

So, as a business, you'll be collecting GST for the government. Any GST you pay for equipment, manufacturing, or any other business activities, can be deducted from the GST you collect. Office equipment and machinery can all have GST 'deducted' or counted against the GST you take from customers. You are required to keep records, and to fill in a Business Activity Statement (BAS) and send it to the Tax Office.

The extra paperwork can be expensive in terms of time and wages, so it is important to set up a simple and efficient GST accounting system. When it is time to fill in your BAS you want it to be quick and painless, and there are many powerful accounting computer programs available to help you. It's worth a little pain to build a solid foundation so that the ongoing process is easy.

Registering for GST

If you're a small sole trader and you make less than $50 000 a year at your business, you don't have to register for GST. You can sell goods and services and not charge GST. This eliminates the hassle of collecting and passing on GST, not to mention all the paperwork.

But there are some downsides. You can't deduct any GST you pay for equipment, materials or anything else. If you buy a fromulating machine for $1100, you've lost $100 GST. Also, some potential customers may not want to deal with you. The law says that they have to pay 48.5 per cent of the money they owe you to the Tax Office (that's the highest tax rate). The Tax Office holds this money for you until the end of the financial year, and then calculates your total tax and gives you a refund if applicable. So you could sell widgets to Acme Machines Pty Ltd for $100. They would be forced by law to give you just $51.50, and $48.50 to the Tax Office.

As you can see, even if you are a small business making less than $50 000, you may want to register for GST. You simply apply to the Tax Office for an Australian Business Number (ABN) and you'll be collecting and charging GST.

Because tax law changes often (usually making it more complicated) it's a good idea to keep up to date with current laws. See the Australian Tax Office website (www.ato.gov.au) for assistance.

The share market

There's a powerful, alien beast that lives deep in the heart of the financial world. It destroys individuals, and big and small companies alike. When the beast is feeling generous, it rewards with enormous wealth. It's called many things by many people. Bourse, Dow, CAC, FTSE, Hang Seng, SBC ... Whatever the local name, most will recognise it as the share market.

It's not really a beast, though it does have a life of its own. That life comes from investors and their perception of the share market.

So what exactly *is* the share market?

For most people the share market is a big mystery. On TV or in the movies, a bunch of people in funny-coloured shirts and waistcoats shout and make bizarre hand-gestures. Computer monitors spew out cryptic messages ... WAG, SSS, ZAL, GOD, PIE, 202 +2, 1020 +11 ... It's enough to scare anybody.

The share market is simply a way to trade wealth, or potential wealth. You can make or lose money on the trade itself, and on the use of the items traded. It's called a 'share' market because pieces or shares of companies are bought and sold. We use the terms 'stock' and 'shares' interchangeably in this book. The letters that you see on the monitors are short codes for the names of companies; the numbers are the prices of the stocks and the most recent change, whether it is up or down.

You may already be an investor in the share market and not even know. Most superannuation funds invest your money; usually some will be in cash (for the interest), some in property (for rental fees and profit from sales), and some in shares (for profits); or even a combination of all three.

Why do companies offer shares?

Companies sell shares to get *capital*, or cash. They might want to expand (buy more equipment, employ more people, buy another company) or pay off some debts.

Let's say your friend Darren has started a new company, DarCom, writing and selling high-tech custom software for large companies. DarCom sales are up and the first few years in business are profitable. But Darren needs to expand the operation and hire more software engineers, research his next product and buy new computers. He could get a loan, or he could sell part of the company.

If Darren applies for a loan, the bank will only lend him a few hundred thousand dollars, and he'd have to pay it back out of profits. If there's trouble in the future, Darren might not be able to make the loan payments and he could lose his company.

Alternatively Darren can sell part of the company. By doing this he can potentially raise millions without having to pay anything back! Of course, his investors will own a piece of the profits, but his profits will increase, so Darren won't really be losing anything.

How it works

Darren decides to 'go public' and make a public share offering, or an *initial public offer* (IPO). Darren tells you about the company and his plans to *float*. He gives you a *prospectus*, a document detailing the offer. The prospectus has to meet certain legal requirements of the Australian Securities and Investments Commission (ASIC), the government body that regulates shares and trading. It's labelled with a disclaimer that says the information could be wrong or biased, and that all investors are responsible for their own decisions. ASIC tries to keep every company honest, but in the end, it *is* a sales document, designed to get you excited about buying.

Darren tells you how successful the company is, and how smart it would be to own a piece of it. If his company continues to be successful there will be a higher demand for a piece of the action and the share price will go up. When that happens, you can sell some of your shares and make a profit. You could also hold onto the shares and get paid a portion of the company profits — that's what *dividends* are.

It sounds like a good investment so you whip out your chequebook. How much should you spend? Darren's Board of Directors (the elected people who help him run the company), the company accountants and a stockbroker worked out that since Darren needed about $2 million worth of new equipment and staff, they would offer 1 million shares at $2 each.

You decide to buy 2500 shares and write a cheque for $5000. You fill in a form in the prospectus Darren gave you, which assures ASIC that you have read the prospectus and understand the warnings.

Now you just sit back and wait for the profit!

Darren is a good salesman; he sells many of the shares

himself. But to make sure they are all sold, he has found an *underwriter*, who will guarantee to take a large chunk in return for a fee. The underwriter is often a firm of stock brokers who will sell the shares to its top clients and set up the Stock Exchange listing.

As it turns out, DarCom is *oversubscribed*. That means there are more people who want to buy shares than there are shares. This is good for the company — it means all the shares will be sold. (If a company is undersubscribed the entire float is in jeopardy.)

The underwriter offers the shares to its own clients first. Any that are not sold are then offered to other people who filled out the prospectus form. They are chosen by when they subscribed and how many shares they want. It's an attempt to be fair, but some people are left out, and their money is returned. You got in early so you've been accepted. You now own 2500 shares of DarCom.

DarCom will pay a dividend twice a year. The dividend has been set at eight cents (for now), so eight cents multiplied by your original 2500 gives you $200 for doing nothing!

A year goes by and DarCom is making a healthy profit. People really want to buy shares. DarCom shares are trading publicly on the stock exchange for $3! If you sell them now, you'd get $7500. $7500 minus the original $5000 equals $2500 gross profit. You'd be giving up the dividends, but then, DarCom can change the dividend and even stop issuing dividends at any time. You decide to sell.

You use a stockbroker to sell your shares. He or she matches your 'sell' order with a 'buy' order. One of their clients wants DarCom and is looking to buy shares; they will pay anything from $2.90 to $3.10. The client believes the shares will keep climbing and they want to get in while they can. Your broker negotiates with their client and you get $3.10 per share, or $7750, minus his commission.

Important points

The DarCom example is simplified. For a start, it's unlikely anyone is going to walk up to you and offer you shares to buy. To find out what's going on in the share market and to find out about new companies and new offers, you need to look in publications like *Shares* or the *Australian Financial Review*. The Australian Stock Exchange (ASX) website also has listings (www.asx.com.au). Also, a stockbroker could keep you informed about upcoming floats.

> Be careful when looking at a potential company. If the float is to raise money for expansion — great. But if the company is trying to pay off debt, stay away.
>
> There's more to setting the price and under-writing. In fact, very complicated calculations are used.

The most important point to consider is about the trading in the future. A company that offers shares is usually only interested in the money from the initial public offer. After that, the company doesn't get any more money from the shares. The shareholders are actually a bit of a thorn in the company's side. They have voting rights on major decisions that affect the business, they scream for dividends, and they can cause chaos by buying and selling shares.

For example, say DarCom is making big profits and the share price goes up because investors want to own this stock. The price hits $5 a share. In some ways, this affects DarCom's worth, because the share value is part of figuring out how much a company would be worth if it was sold. But in another way, it really has nothing to do with the company. The same people work at DarCom Monday to Friday, presumably doing a competent job on any given day, but because investors want more shares, the price goes up, as if the company and people had improved.

This is extremely important because it is the heart of how the share market operates. To some degree, it doesn't matter if a company is run well, 'worth' a lot of money, or not worth anything. Shares, once on the stock exchange, work entirely on perception and demand. Investors think/feel a certain stock is valuable and scramble to buy it, and that drives the price even higher.

Investors base their decisions on many indicators: company reports, press releases to brokers and the public, and the market in general. How accurate this information is doesn't really matter. It's all about what people believe.

It can go bad, too. Say Darren's friend, Melinda, is the accountant. She's doing a fine job. But a few years ago there was a problem with the books where Melinda used to work. Melinda's reputation has been hurt by this and an investor has found out. Even though Melinda is actually doing a competent job, her past reputation is perceived by the public as bad. They think that DarCom is using a dishonest accountant or an idiot to keep the books. Suddenly people can't unload the shares fast enough. The price drops more, the shares get even harder to sell and the price drops more ...

Yet it's still the same people at DarCom, with the same skills and, apart from the perception problem, the company is healthy. Here's another way to look at it: the shares affect the company, the company does not affect the shares (much).

That is worth repeating: shareholders and their perception change the price of the shares. The company does not change the price of the shares *directly*.

Technically, though, the company can *influence* the

price. When Darren hired his old friend Melinda, the effect was that the shares went down. But it could easily have gone unnoticed. Darren could announce a new product with great potential and the shares could go up. It's not so much what the company does, but how *shareholders react*.

A very common scenario is profit disappointment. A company announces projected quarterly or yearly profits, and when the date rolls around profits are good, but not quite as good as projected. The shareholders see this as a huge failure and they start selling shares, forcing the share price down, which starts a domino effect. The company has made a very healthy profit, and if the company had announced a smaller projection, and met or exceeded it, shareholders probably would have been very happy and driven the price up!

You may be thinking that companies should reduce all projected targets so shareholders will be happier when the targets are easily met. It probably happens. But too small a target looks like too little growth, which shareholders can also perceive as bad.

What good are shares?

When you own a share, you own part of a company. You have a say in how the company is managed. This doesn't mean you can barge into the boardroom and tell them how to run things, but it does allow you to vote on issues the board of directors proposes at an annual general meeting (AGM). The company can also call a meeting if there's an important decision to be made that affects shareholders. Your say is based on the number of shares you have. Obviously the bigger the number of shares, the more influence you'll have.

You can vote on re-electing directors, how much

directors are paid, allowing an employee share plan or dividend reinvestment plan, or more serious issues affecting the future of the company, like accepting a takeover bid or purchasing other companies.

(Note: You can get a tax deduction for attending an AGM, but there are severe restrictions.)

Show me the money

But when it comes down to it, you bought shares for the money. Depending on how the company operates (and of course on whether it actually makes a profit) it has to share the profits with its investors each year. These payments are generally called *dividends*, but can also be called *distributions* or *payments*. Dividends are paid to the shareholders either annually, bi-annually or quarterly. The amount is determined by the company. They may choose to put some or all of the profits back into the business to help it to grow, or distribute a major chunk back to the shareholders to keep them happy. The money is usually distributed per share, so the more shares you have, the more dividends you get.

The other major benefit is that you can buy and sell shares, which is called *trading*. The obvious trick is to buy them for a little and sell them for a lot.

The stock exchange

The stock exchange is the place where all the share trading is recorded. The first stock exchanges grew when traders and merchants made deals. They kept track of their deals with accounts, which in a way were 'exchanges' of goods and money, hence the name. France had a sort of exchange in the late 1100s. Later in the 1500s and 1600s other countries in Europe started their own exchanges. Business went wild.

Credit and capital were needed. Banks and shares came alive.

These days the Australian Stock Exchange (ASX) is computerised. Buy and Sell orders are linked in the official system called *Stock Exchange Automated Trading System* (SEATS). In the old days, however (and in many other countries today), trades were made manually on a floor with paper.

To complete the transaction the *Clearing House Electronic Sub-register System* (CHESS) is used. This records all the share sales, so there's no need to send paperwork between the Stock Exchange and brokers.

All ordinary

To gauge how healthy a stock exchange is on any one day, the top companies' share prices are added up and used as an *index* or indicator. In Australia there are several indices, but the main index is called the All Ordinaries. If, out of the thousands of companies out there, the top 500 companies' shares are performing well, then we say that the market is healthy. For example, if the 'All Ords' opens at 2946 on Monday morning, and the index companies' share prices rise, it might close at 2972, up 26 points. Some of those individual company shares may have gone down, and some up, but on the whole the gains were more than the losses.

The All Ords has now changed, and the modern index used in Australia is the S&P/ASX 200. This is the Standard & Poor index combined with the Australian Stock Exchange (ASX) list of 200 companies. Some other indices are sector specific.

If the All Ords index keeps rising, investors are optimistic. If it keeps dropping, though, they're pessimistic. But does it really translate directly to any concrete action or result?

Some people would say no. Remember perception and the DarCom example? In that example the staff were the same on Friday as on Monday, but when shareholders perceived a bright future the shares went up. They perceived a bad future and the shares dropped ... it's the same with any index. It doesn't necessarily translate to anything useful. Still, if the All Ords drops 200 points, it's good bet that many companies, as well as the economy in general, are hurting.

How investors make a profit

There are many different investing methods and systems, but they all fall under one of two schools of logic, and they both try to follow the old advice of 'buy low, sell high'. It sounds simple but the tricky part is knowing *when* to buy and when to sell. Hunches and feelings are unreliable.

Gamblers and gardeners

The exciting and risky school is aimed at fast profit. These investors are *gamblers* or *cowboys*. They buy shares at a low price and sell them at a higher price, picking up dividends in between. Gamblers aren't particularly interested in dividends, though the extra profit is good. Gamblers often operate short-term and watch for active periods where their target stocks fluctuate wildly. Get in, get out.

This type of investing requires a lot of knowledge and experience to make dangerous but informed gambles. Gamblers spend a lot of time studying the market and the factors affecting it. Still, their main key to success is luck. Studies show that generally, gamblers make a lot of profit, but there's a 'but'. You knew it ... only a few are successful. Most gamblers lose. They may buy a lot of one stock, hoping it will rise, only to have it stay steady or fall. Of course, when they *are* successful, they are *very* successful.

The other type of investing is a safer, less exciting style — diversification. To reduce risk, investors don't put all their eggs in one basket. They spread their money across several companies and types of companies (*sectors*). If one company makes a loss, others are probably making a profit. It's a balance, with the goal being to come out a little bit ahead.

These investors are called *gardeners* or *farmers*. It's because they nurture their safe investments. They work hard at research and are prepared to wait for profit. Gardeners have a higher chance of making money than gamblers. Gardeners don't make as much short-term profit as gamblers might, but in the long run they are usually more successful.

All that said, everyone gets lucky breaks and bad breaks. The problem with gambling is that it's very risky and requires knowledge and energy. The problem with gardening is that if you diversify too much, all the profits are eaten by all the losses.

Balance is the key. And luck.

Sectors

To diversify, investors put money into different types of companies, or business sectors: alcohol (beer, wine, spirits), building (commercial, residential), finance (banks, insurance), resources (chemical/mining/energy), etc. These sectors have been officially re-classed into broad, worldwide categories called GICS (Global Industry Classification Standards):

Energy
Materials
Industrials
Consumer Discretionary

Consumer Staples
Healthcare
Financials (including property trusts)
Financials (not including property trusts)
Property Trusts
Information Technology
Telecommunication
Utilities

Many investors pick one sector that's on the rise; they invest in the leading manufacturer and all the *competing* manufacturers in a category. This is not true diversification because it's concentrating on one category, but it does have benefits. Don't be loyal in investing. If you love Acme brand coffee, sure, invest in it, but also invest in healthy competitors.

Managed funds

One way to be a safe gardener is to invest in managed funds. These are huge *investment portfolios*, or collections of investments, managed by a bank or other financial institution. Instead of researching what sectors and what companies you should invest in, you can use someone else's experience to do all the work. Unlike a sharebroker, an entire organisation is devoted to investing your money (and lots of other people's) in thousands of different types of shares and property. You can choose from safe investments with moderate profit, aggressive investments (fancy way to say 'risky'), or a combination of the two. You can even limit yourself to 'green' companies.

Good things about managed funds

1   They are generally safe
2   Someone else does it all for you

3   They are all very diversified
4   Some funds invest in futures, warrants and property

Bad things about managed funds

1   They are not always as safe as they seem (everyone loses at times)
2   You have little control
3   Fees (entry, exit and management) are often high
4   Profit is generally mild

If you're already rich and need to keep your money machine working, a managed fund is good. It's not a great way to *get* rich, but is a good way to get your feet wet. Many superannuation funds are just a type of managed fund, and this can be a good way to get some exposure to investing.

Like a bank

Many amateur investors use shares as forced savings or putting money away for a rainy day. The money is locked up in shares so that it's not instantly accessible, but the shares can be usually cashed in just by calling a broker. A wise investor who has chosen correctly may even get a better return on their investment than if they'd put the money into a term deposit at a bank.

You can also save on fees by having your money in shares instead of a bank. You only pay the broker a fee when you buy or sell shares and there are no nasty monthly bank fees draining away your investment. Other than the tax on dividends (see the franking section on page 116 to learn about wonderful things like *imputation credits*), you only pay tax on the shares if you make a profit on them (a *capital gain*), and then only when you sell them. Currently, if you hold the shares for over one year you only pay the tax on *half* your capital gain, which is even better. This means that you have some control over what tax you pay and when.

The other advantage is that unlike depositing your money into an investment account, you can choose from so many companies on the Stock Exchange that you can really diversify.

Unlike a bank

Everything above is true, but not always. It can also be *very dangerous* to treat the share market like a bank. While shares and the market in general go up and down, banks have some capital or money guarantees. You can't lose everything. If you keep your shares long enough you may come out ahead 20 years later, but you could easily be wiped out. There are no guarantees.

Here's a true story. Lots of people bought shares in a big insurance company, an Australian icon (no names, please). The shares soared high. Some people sold at the peak and made amazing profits. Many kept the shares to use for their children's education in the future, thinking they would always be worth a lot. Unfortunately, the shares dropped so severely they became almost worthless. The company itself now has major financial and management troubles.

Worse, many shareholders are determined to keep the shares and wait it out, hoping the value of their shares will rise again. Realistically, it may be years before the shares recover. This was a case of shareholders being emotional and not understanding the share market.

Dividends

Dividends are one of the great beauties of owning shares — to get unearned income and keep your money machine rolling. Dividends or payable company profits are set by the company. The company might decide to stop issuing dividends for a time, or reduce the amount. Some company shares do not entitle holders to dividends at all. Be wary if the company has to take out a loan to pay dividends — it's a sign of financial trouble. This would be disclosed in the annual report.

Franking

In the past, companies paid taxes on their profits, then distributed part of the profits to shareholders as dividends. The shareholders then had to pay tax on the dividends. Effectively, the government got double tax.

These days, however, companies receive a tax credit when they pay tax, and they can pass this on to the shareholder. The dividend is called a *franked dividend* and the tax credit you receive is called the *dividend imputation* or *imputation credit*.

Technically, the franked dividend is not tax-free to the shareholder, it's a credit applied to tax. It works like this: DarCom makes a distribution profit of $100 000. It pays its tax of 30 per cent (the corporate tax rate) or $30 000, so there's $70 000 left to distribute to shareholders. There are one million shares, so your holdings of 2500 shares equal a franked dividend of $175 ($0.07 per share). In this case DarCom is paying all the tax up-front, so it's a fully franked dividend.

Not all dividends are franked. Some are partially franked or not franked at all. It makes a big difference to your profit, so examine potential dividends carefully.

For tax purposes you are recorded as having received the full pre-tax dividend, called the *grossed-up* dividend, of $250 ($0.10 per share) and a *franking credit* of $75 ($0.03 per share). Because dividends are a kind of income, your own income tax rate is applied to the grossed-up amount. So, say your income tax rate is 42 per cent, then you would owe 42 per cent of the $250, which is $105. You then take away the amount of your franking credit ($75) and you only owe $30. If you were on a tax rate of 30 per cent, you wouldn't have to pay any more tax. If you were on a tax rate of less than 30 per cent, you would come out ahead with credit left over, and you could apply this to other specific types of income (the Tax Office can advise you of the limitations).

According to financial professionals, franked dividends can be worth more than simple bank interest. This is because of the tax credit. Even if you only get a partial benefit from the franking, you'll generally come out ahead compared to people who only earn bank interest. Of course, it does depend on the interest rate.

CGT — find out what it means to me

When you sell shares, any profit you have gained is taxed by the capital gains tax (CGT). You knew it would be taxed, right?

CGT isn't as bad as it sounds, although it can be complicated. To maximise benefits you might have to pre-plan big share purchases and get professional advice. Tax law changes fast, so keep up to date through an accountant.

Before CGT was introduced your share gains were taxed as straight profit, part of your regular income. Now, CGT only taxes a *portion* of the profit. (Note that your gains can still be taxed fully if the Tax Office thinks you are a professional investor.) You must own shares for at least one year to get the CGT benefit, otherwise you'll have to pay full tax on your gain.

There's been an ongoing battle in most modern countries over CGT. The idea is that shares should be taxed only a little to encourage investing and stimulate the economy. Others say, 'Tax those rich investors!' Australia has had CGT since 1985. CGT rules change with govern-ments, but currently only 50 per cent of the profit is taxed.

So, for example, what if you bought Acme shares at $4 a share, and the price *dropped*? This is a capital *loss*, and is not taxable. The loss can be used to reduce your tax, though. You can apply the loss from one share deal to a gain on another. Remember those franking credits? Let's say you came out way ahead and had some extra credits but didn't know what to do with them ... you could apply them to a capital gain and reduce your tax on it.

Losses and gains can often be carried over to the next year's tax, or used to offset other investments. It's very important to get current advice from an accountant or tax specialist. There are different methods for calculating CGT (the discount and the index). Go to the Tax Office website for the latest rulings and details (www.ato.gov.au).

Different types of investment on the stock market

Ordinary shares

These are exactly what they sound like; plain, ordinary shares. They are the most common and the most basic. They often pay dividends, but not always. They come with voting rights, and you can pick and choose when you'll sell them. They generally don't have restrictions.

Blue chip shares

A blue chip share is a share of any company that is huge, stable and old, and usually worth a lot, the sort of company that makes you think they will be in business forever, and that if they do go under you will look at getting off the planet because everything will be in the toilet. But blue chips are not indestructible. Some of the big ones have crashed.

The name 'blue chip' comes from casino chips, when the most valuable chip was blue. Local blue chips include BHP, NewsCorp and Telstra. They are in the Top 50 companies (usually part of any index), and are often reported in the financial news.

Blue chips are often expensive to buy and yield little growth, but pay steady dividends.

Preference shares

Preference shares are shares that pay at a fixed dividend rate, which is usually a percentage of their value. The preference part comes into it if the company goes bad: these shares get paid out before, or 'in preference' to, ordinary shares; handy when a company is running low on money.

Contributing shares

These are only partly paid for; they need further future payments at certain times.

Options

Options are vouchers to purchase shares at a fixed price, usually a discount on the market price at the time the options are issued. You can get different types of options in different ways. When you buy shares they sometimes come with free-attaching options. Some employee share plans also offer options.

Company issued options

These are common and straightforward. A company issues options to existing shareholders or employee shareholders, and when the options are used or *exercised*, new shares are created by the company. The company itself gets the money, rather than a public shareholder in the share market.

Say DarCom has decided to give all the shareholders some company-issued options. The current share price is $3, so DarCom sets the option *exercise price* at $2.50. To exercise them you pay $2.50 for new shares that are currently worth $3. You can then sell the new shares and make a $0.50 per share gross profit.

Not a bad deal, but it gets better. You can often sell the options themselves. If they're *listed options*, meaning they are listed on the share market, they can be traded publicly. Unlisted options can only be traded privately, if at all, depending on restrictions. Various restrictions can apply to both listed and unlisted options.

The option trading price on the share market is determined by supply and demand, and the difference between the exercise price and the current market price for the shares. You're essentially buying and selling a discount voucher, so obviously the price can't go too high, otherwise the option buyer will end up paying almost the full share price to exercise the options.

Options have an expiry date, usually a few years from the issue date, but this varies. If they are not exercised, they become worthless. Sometimes there are other restrictions. You might have to wait until a particular date before you can exercise the options, or there may be several start and end dates, so you'd have to exercise the options in lots.

Let's say that you've kept the DarCom options instead of selling. The exercise date is two years from the date they were issued. A year goes by; DarCom is financially healthy and the shares are trading at $4. This is very good for you. You can pay $2.50 to exercise the options to buy more shares, and then sell the new shares at around $4, a 60 per cent profit of $1.50!

But you decide to wait another year. Sadly, by then DarCom shares are trading at $2.35. The general market and DarCom's good health tell you that the share price will probably eventually go back up. But the option expiry is close by and you can't wait. What to do?

You could still exercise the options and take a gamble that the shares will go back up. Since you're paying more for the shares than they are currently worth, you're taking a chance that you will lose. To compensate for the risk you may have to increase your profit goal:

Current share price	$2.35
Option exercise price	$2.50
Immediate loss	$0.15
Break-even sell price	$2.50
Original target sell price	$4.00
Compensated target sell	$4.15
	(or more)

With the above example you could sell any time the shares got above $2.50 and still make a profit. If everything looks healthy for the future, you could risk holding on beyond that point in case the shares climb more. But the compensated target sell price you set is artificial. It's old, related to the original target when the shares were worth a lot more — the shares might not get that high for years. It would be safer to make a new goal of say, $2.75–3.

You could also allow the options to lapse. Since the options were a gift from the company you haven't lost anything, you just haven't gained. Options can be a way to gamble safely. If the shares climb you can exercise the options; if the shares drop you've only lost the option price.

Exchange traded options

Exchange traded options (ETOs) are much more complex, partly because they are traded publicly like shares. Instead of thinking of them simply as discount vouchers, it's more accurate to think of them as discount voucher *contracts*. You set a price and conditions. ETOs are for shares that already exist — the company doesn't get any money.

The Australian Stock Exchange (ASX) advises new investors to gain experience before attempting to trade in ETOs. These options offer benefits, but only if the investor knows the rules and limitations.

To find out about ETOs, call options, put options and protected writes, visit the ASX web site (www.asx.com.au).

Warrants

Warrants are like exchange traded options, but with many technical differences. These differences actually make warrants more like shares than options. Warrants have a much longer expiry period than options, and they are created or issued by financial institutions. The institutions are sometimes banks, and are approved but not guaranteed by the ASX.

All the warnings for ETOs also apply to warrants. Learn more from the ASX website, and gain some experience before warrant trading.

Futures

Futures are contracts to buy or sell a particular asset on a set date in the future. They are traded over commodities such as wool, oil, gold and grain, and they are traded on their own Futures Exchange rather than on the Stock Exchange.

Many investors trade futures to invest in sectors easily. For example, if you thought the future was in gold, you could either buy shares in the dozens of companies that mine gold, or you could just buy gold mining futures. You're betting that gold will go up by the time the contract is due. If it does, you'll make money. If it doesn't, you'll lose. Futures, even with supporting information, are a gamble.

Interest rate securities

An interest rate security is almost like having a term deposit in a bank, except they can be traded in the same way as shares. There's a set term, and when it's due the company will repay you the value of the security. In the meantime, the company pays you a dividend or interest rate based on a specific rate per year. You're guaranteed a fixed return. With ordinary shares you don't know how much the dividend will be (it can change), if there'll even be one, or how long it will last. The share can also drop in price. There are no big gains, but a steady known return.

Free shares

Believe it or not, sometimes you *can* get money for nothing. Aside from unearned income, there are rare instances where you can get shares or options for nothing (or at a great discount).

Employee share plans

Some companies offer an *employee share plan*, or ESP, to their staff. It's a good idea from the company's point of view, because it can create a greater sense of team spirit and loyalty, and an interest in making sure the company remains strong and profitable. The employees can trade the shares and make money (although sometimes time restrictions are put in place to protect the company). Some share plans are cancelled if the employee leaves the company. It depends on how generous the company is, and on tax implications.

Employee shares are often given at a discount on the share price at the time they are issued. There are many complicated tax laws governing how much can be given before the tax man taketh away, so ESPs differ greatly. A lot of people are cautious about taking employee shares because they get confused about the tax issues. The company should be able to help you to understand the tax implications, so despite small hassles, employee share plans are a great opportunity to get your feet wet in the share market. You can gain experience, and you might even make a profit! (Remember, though, even your own company's shares can go down; none of our examples allow for that!)

Instead of dreading the thought of complex taxes, talk to the company. If necessary, hire a professional, registered tax accountant. It's often under $100 and it's even tax deductible. If the numbers work, go for it.

Tax deferred shares

Employee shares can be *tax deferred*, which means that you get the shares now and you pay tax on the shares when you sell them. That sounds fantabulous, but it's not always! If you buy shares with money you have already paid tax on, your share profit will have the benefit of capital gains tax (only part of the profit is taxed if you have held the shares for more than one year). But if the shares are tax deferred, because your money was not taxed at the start, when you sell and count your profit it's all added to your entire income and taxed, without gaining the CGT benefit. The tax *can* work out to be much higher, but not always. Every plan is different.

Cashing in the shares during a low income period in

your life (maternity leave, unemployment, retirement, etc.) can be a major benefit. The share profit will be added to your annual income and taxed fully, but if you haven't made much in wages you won't be taxed much. Another benefit is that you have more upfront cash to buy more shares. More shares means more dividends.

There are many variables, so do the maths. Here's just one example (simplified with easy tax amounts, these may differ in real life):

Standard taxed example

You work for DarCom and earn $1000 per week gross ($52 000 per year). After tax you take home $761. DarCom shares are selling at $1. You decide to buy shares as just a regular shareholder. You take a week's pay and buy 761 shares. One year later the shares are worth $1.25 and you decide to sell.

761 shares @ $1.25	$951.25
Gross share profit ($951.25 – $761.00)	190.25
Taxable share profit (CGT 50% × $190.25)	95.13
Tax ($95.13 × 42%)	39.95
Net share profit ($190.25 – $39.95)	150.30
Taxable dividend ($0.10 per share × 12 months)	76.10
Tax ($76.10 × 42%)	31.96
Net dividend profit	44.14
Share + dividend profit	194.44
Your $1000 has become (after taxes)	$955.44

Tax deferred example

You take a week's pay and buy shares under the employee tax-deferred plan. Instead of 761 shares, you can buy 1000 (gross pay multiplied by share price). One year later the shares are higher and you sell. (Note: The year you bought the shares you earned less, so you paid less tax; the year you sold the shares you earned your regular pay plus the share profit, paying more tax. Trust us, this is figured into the example.)

1000 shares @ $1.25	$1250.00
Gross profit	1250.00
Net profit (minus your $1000 gross pay)	250.00
Tax (on difference between tax years)	325.00
Net share profit (shares minus balanced tax)	163.25
Taxable dividend ($0.10 per share × 12 months)	100.00
Tax ($100 × 42%)	42.00
Net dividend profit	58.00
Net share profit + dividend profit	221.25
Your $1000 has become (after taxes)	$983.00

The tax-deferred example puts you slightly ahead. If you sold the shares during a low income year you would be even further ahead in the transaction (although you would have earned less in the year). The major benefit in the example is dividends: you have more! If you are in the top tax bracket, a deferred plan means you can buy about twice as many shares compared to just buying shares out of your wage.

Your own example will be different. We've assumed some generic tax rates and have hidden the complex calculation for the 'short-wage' year and the extra year.

Tax exempt shares

Depending on the company and the employee share plan, you can also get some shares for free, that are also tax exempt! The amount varies with a change in government, but is generally $1000 worth of shares tax-free. You wouldn't have to pay for the shares, and you wouldn't have to pay tax on them. However, you *would* have to pay tax on the *profit* if you sell the shares.

The Tax Office won't let you be in a tax-deferred and tax-exempt plan at the same time.

Option plans

Employee share plans for options are also available. Options are a great way to take a chance on shares without outlaying the full value of the shares and risking a huge loss. The employee option plan may set the exercise price at a discount as with normal options, but because of the plan rules and the tax allowances, this can sometimes mean a greater discount than getting standard options in the company.

Employee option plans can have restrictions; it depends on the particular plan and what taxation allowances the company was able to make with the Tax Office. Standard options give you more flexibility to watch the market, but may not have the tax and discount benefits.

Options can be a way to save on broker fees!

Bonus shares

Bonus shares are free! They're offered to current shareholders at no cost. Usually this means that the value of the shares is spread across the new investment total.

Say you have 1000 shares in DarCom at $2 each. DarCom has a bonus issue at one share for every five shares you hold (1:5). Your shareholding has increased by 200 shares, so you now have 1200 shares in DarCom. But the value of the shares has dropped or been diluted. The overall total is the same ($1000 \times \$2 = \$2000$), but each share is now worth $1.66 instead of $2. You gain more shares, but not more value. The advantage is, however, that if the shares climb, you've got more potential profit — and of course, more dividends (and you didn't even pay for them!)

Remember that this value is theoretical: your investment can also decrease. If the market reacts by seeing the bonus issue as watering down the company's shares, the shares could drop. And here's where it can get complicated. A drop could actually be the reason for the bonus issue! Because if the shares are trading at too high an individual price, investors may be reluctant to invest in the company. The company attempts to solve this by lowering the individual share *price*, but not the *value*.

Rights issues

Rights issues are just like bonus issues, except that you have to pay for them. Usually they're offered at a discount. This is another way for a company to make more money from shares after they have been listed on the Stock Exchange.

A big advantage of rights issues is that you don't have to pay any brokerage fees. However, new shares can cause the share price to drop. As with any share purchase or investment deal, check the numbers and see if they work for you before you buy.

If the company is using the additional funds created by the issue to fund expansion and growth, then the share price may rise, especially if there will be dividends. But if the company needs the money to pay off debts, it could be a bad sign. You also need to watch the market price during the rights issue. If the shares drop below the issue price, it may not be worth taking up the offer at all.

There are two types of rights issues.

Renounceable rights issue

This means you can sell your entitlement to participate in the rights issue on the share market. The value of your entitlement is worked out in theory using the difference between the market value of the shares on the market, and the price set to purchase the shares via the rights issue. Say the rights issue price was $1.75 and the market price was $2. You could sell each entitlement for a share at $0.25 depending on market fluctuations.

Once you sell your entitlement, it's gone to another investor. You can't purchase any shares with it. Of course this also means that if you wanted to buy more shares than your entitlement allowed, you could buy more entitlements on the market yourself.

Non-renounceable rights issue

This means that you can't sell your entitlement. You can either take up the rights issue or ignore it.

Share purchase plan

These are very similar to a rights issue, except that you're not issued with 'rights'; you are simply offered shares (sometimes a specific number of shares) in the company at a specific price.

And a cherry on top

When you look at any issue a company offers you, see if there are any other advantages besides the share price discount and avoidance of brokerage fees. Some companies offer extra benefits. You may be able to pick up free attaching options when you purchase more shares, or the type of shares you're offered might be different, such as preference shares or interest-bearing securities that may only be offered to existing shareholders.

Any company offer is *definitely* worth a look. Crunch the numbers and see if it's worth the cost/risk. Thoroughly read any explanatory material, and take the company offer of help. Talk to the Tax Office and if necessary get outside expert advice. If it is all worth it for you, then make sure you send in the application well before the deadline — sometimes these offers operate on a first-come, first-served basis.

Dividend reinvestment plans

Often companies will offer extra shares to shareholders by giving them the opportunity to reinvest their dividends in shares, rather than taking the dividends as cash. These are known as dividend reinvestment plans, or DRPs. This means you can gain extra shares without paying any brokerage fees. Usually the company will also offer a discount on the shares on the market price, at anything up to 10 per cent, to encourage shareholders to participate. On top of all that, the dividends are distributed *after* the company has paid its tax, so the shares are franked — that means they come with dividend imputation credits.

If you can afford to give up the cash dividend and want to increase your shareholding, DRPs are great. The only disadvantage is that you have to keep good records of each DRP share purchase, because each purchase will be on a different date; working out any capital gain or loss when you sell the shares at a later date will be a bit involved. However, that's a minor complication as you should *always* keep good records! (Not just for your own convenience, but the Tax Office gets excited in a bad way when you don't.)

Another type of dividend reinvestment is called a bonus share scheme. In this case you're paid the dividend in shares rather than cash, but for tax purposes it's treated more like a bonus issue. The shares you get instead of dividends are considered to have been acquired on the same date as your original shares. This *can* be a tax advantage, but it depends on what the acquisition price was when you bought the original shares. You also don't receive any tax credits with this type of scheme.

Takeovers

Takeovers can be very intricate, and they're subject to complex laws. They occur when a company (or a rich individual) buys enough shares in another company to be able to control it. The buyer generally needs around 50 per cent of the shares to gain control of the company. They can then influence the board, and therefore the company's direction, through management decisions. Sometimes they may only need around 30 per cent of the shares, because it's unlikely that the other shareholders will band together and fight. This really depends on company structure and what percentage is needed for major votes. Most takeover bids try to gain 100 per cent the company eventually.

There are laws in place to help prevent 'hostile' takeovers (in which there is no formal takeover offer). For example, you can't hold more than 5 per cent of a company's shareholding without declaring a *substantial shareholding*. If someone wants to go to 20 per cent or above, they need either to make a formal takeover offer ('I am trying to buy the company!'), or increase their shareholding in increments of only 3 per cent every six months. Alternatively they can gain the shares under approval by the shareholders at a meeting.

Who cares if the company is taken over? The shareholders do! A takeover can be a great way to make money. Shareholders are often offered extra cash, shares, or a combination of both. The offer is usually made above the current share market value.

Offers can either come through a broker, or directly to

shareholders from the company who wants to buy the shares. The company being considered for takeover may also send out information, explaining whether they are 'for' or 'against' the takeover. If you have a shareholding that receives a takeover offer, make sure you read everything carefully before you make your decision. It can turn out to be a bad deal, too.

Obviously if the bidder doesn't gain enough shares to take over the company, the takeover will fail. If they gain 90 per cent of the shares they need, with more than 75 per cent of the shareholders accepting, then the offer is known as being 'unconditional'. This means that even if you didn't want to accept the offer you will still have your shares bought out.

Buybacks

Companies can offer to buy shares back from their share-holders. They might feel the shares are undervalued, they might want to prevent the shares from being vulnerable to a takeover, or they might want to raise the company's own shareholding to increase control. If the shares have dropped in price many shareholders may no longer have a 'marketable parcel' of shares (enough to be practical), and these shareholders may be offered a buyback.

Buybacks only happen with shareholder approval and the financial ability to pay for the bought-back shares, and the restriction on the number of shares the company can hold must also be met.

Any offer needs to be judged on its own merits, but if you're offered a buyback it may save you from holding shares that are undervalued or losing value.

The unsure thing

There are systems and time-tested methods of making wise investment choices, but in the end, it's a gamble. You can do as much research as you want, you can study charts and diagrams and plot trends, but the future is always elusive (except for those lucky people with crystal balls — if you find someone who has one, let us know!) This applies to shares in particular, but also to any investment.

Investment is a gamble because there are many elements that are beyond your control, and many compound outcomes that can't be prefigured. So, no matter how well prepared you are, you can still lose. But you can also win very big, bigger than average. It's truly unpredictable.

Though investing can be a *gamble*, it's very important to not treat it like *gambling*. There's a difference. Even with preparation you might lose; that's the gamble. But without a plan you're just tossing a coin and hoping for the best. You might as well be playing the pokies. Which brings us to common problems you can avoid.

Some people invest in the share market and become addicted, just like betting on horses or pokies. It's not investing to them, it's a game. They love the thrill of winning and the quest for that phantom 'one big deal'. There may be a big win here and there, but there's no magic in investing! It's work.

For others, investments are very personal. They choose companies because they like the name or the colour of the logo, or something else just as superficial. Warm fuzzy feelings have nothing to do with a good investment.

Holding on to falling shares in a dying company because your Great Aunt Zelda gave them to you is taking loyalty too far. Investing is not blindly cheering for the home team. If your investment is not performing properly, you should follow the plan you made at the beginning. You know, the one that said when to buy more and when to sell.

Some investors try to use mind power to influence their investments. They wish and hope. Scientific studies show that it's exactly as effective as yelling at your team on TV, or telling the actor on the screen that the bad guy is around the corner. All this emotional behaviour is very dangerous. You must be unemotional in *all* investment deals. Experienced investors look at an investment merely as numbers in a game.

The most talented cricket batsmen and baseball batters only hit the ball 30 to 50 per cent of the time! They miss the rest of the swings. As an investor, if you can make a profit half the time and lose the other half, you're doing well. How much profit? Experienced traders know it's very difficult to make more than 15 or 20 per cent on a deal.

Stop loss

Experienced investors limit the amount they risk, usually to 1 or 2 per cent of their working money. They have a preset warning bell that tells them to sell, called a *stop loss* in share lingo. If you have $5000 to work with, that means you shouldn't risk more than $100 on a deal. You can *spend* more, but you can't *lose* more.

For example, you want to buy DarCom shares. You can't afford to lose more than $100 on the deal, so if you buy 1000 shares at $1 each ($1000), the shares can't drop more than ten cents (1000 ÷ 100 = 0.10). The ten cents is your stop loss. If the shares drop to 90 cents, you sell. You've *used* $1000 but you've only *risked* (or lost) $100.

Unfortunately, brokerage fees make it worse: you're charged $50 minimum to buy, and you're charged again to sell, making the loss another $100 at least. In this example, you'd have to make your stop loss five cents or buy fewer shares. The good news is that sometimes you can use a discount broker, although certain shares have to be traded by certain full service brokers. (For more on fees and brokers see *Choosing a broker*, page 144.)

The small percentage of 1 to 2 percent may sound conservative, but it's also time-tested. Even a steady share price with low activity and no dividends can cost you: your money is worth less than if it was in the bank earning interest, and it's more at risk.

Any money you invest should be extra money that you can afford to lose. The stop loss is a handy tool, but disaster can always strike before you have a chance to pull out.

Experienced investors build in another layer of complexity when they set a stop loss — market trend indicators. In the above DarCom example, say the price did drop and you did sell. But a few days later the price climbed back to what it was, maybe even a little higher. You'd be kicking yourself because obviously there was simply a company or market glitch; the shares are still healthy. But it would be costly to get back in.

Experienced investors consider the market itself. Is the drop just a temporary bump? It's hard to say. If the price is dropping below a very recent low, or below a trend, they know it's *likely* that the price will keep dropping.

Many shareholders panic at the first price drop and sell, dumping huge share parcels on the market. This causes the price to drop even more, and a domino effect starts. If you wait too long to sell and go far below your stop loss, you can either sell at a huge loss, or try to figure out if the shares will bounce back enough for you to get out with a minimum loss. It's all about timing. Don't just gamble and hope for the best. Use indicators to make an educated decision (see *Picking the winners*, page 136). If the decisions were easy, all shareholders would be rich.

Enough is enough

You also need to know how much profit is enough. (But surely too much is never enough!) If shares keep climbing and climbing, you might be tempted to wait and sell when they peak. But without mind power or science-fiction technology, the only way to see the peak is when it's already happened and the price starts falling. Set an *exit* or *stop gain*; if you sell and the shares go even higher, you haven't lost, you just haven't gained extra. You're safe, and you've made a profit. Knowing when to sell is as difficult as knowing when to buy.

Picking the winners

A lot of factors determine share price, and we can't tell you which shares you should buy. A company might look good on paper, but unexpected events like wars, disasters, weather, or just plain bad management can cause a huge financial loss. If you diversify your investments, over the long term it is possible to invest well in the share market.

It starts with research. What's the market like at the moment? What are people buying and why? If an attractive company has low profits, are there seasonal highs and lows? Is the sales market sustainable? Are there profitable deals in the pipeline? Does the company have good management? There's no easy way to obtain this important information, and no guarantee that the information will be reliable! But you can read trade magazines, financial magazines, check the company press releases (and those of their competitors), and get some advice from a stock broker.

Analyse these

Two time-tested methods of picking a profitable target company are *fundamental* and *technical analysis*. Fundamental analysis involves looking at a company's basic money-making components, or the books and the management. To do this you need to get a copy of the annual report or financial statement — it's free to shareholders and is available upon request for others. Obviously if a company is making a profit (and has assets and a good business plan), it has a good chance of being successful. Still, many healthy companies fail, or perform poorly on the share market.

Technical analysis is plotting the details of share performance. The highs and lows, and the *volume* or number of shares traded, are all recorded by the investor and converted into a chart (bar, line, point-and-figure, candlestick). You can see what the shares are actually doing at a glance. Technical analysis is also called *charting* or *plotting*.

There's great debate about which method is best. Technical fans like the solid feel of accurate, detailed numbers and trend indicators. Fundamental investors like the solid financial information that makes the target company what it is. Both types of analysis are useful. You should use all the tools you can.

Often new investors think they can use technical analysis to predict the future. They look for a pattern and feel sure the shares will rise 25 cents on the second Tuesday in May next year. Technical analysis doesn't work like that.

Charting *can* show trends, even repeating historical trends. But professionals use charting to *confirm* decisions, and to find loose entry and exit windows.

Fundamental tools

Most of the information you'll need can be found in a company's annual report (including the balance sheet and profit and loss statement). Stockbrokers and investment companies can also be a source of information. We'll use DarCom throughout as an example.

Net tangible assets (NTA) or net tangible asset backing (NAB)

This reflects how much a company is worth. Only the physical items after any debts are paid are counted (building, equipment, stock, etc.). Non-physical items like the company name, reputation and expertise are not counted, because they have no specific value. (If the company were sold these items would have a negotiable value.) Debts are subtracted.

$2.5 million assets ÷ 2 million shares = $1.25 per share

Since DarCom shares are trading at $2.50, the company is doing well. Or rather, the market has faith in the company. If the share price was below the NTA, say $0.50, then the market has no confidence in the company. You could see this as a cheap buy, but of course that's only true if the market eventually catches on and the shares do rise.

The NTA is limited, however. The share price doesn't always reflect the true company worth, and assets can be calculated incorrectly (and purposely inflated).

Market capitalisation This is a company's size based on how much the shares are worth.

2 million shares × $2.50 per share = $5 million

Large market capitalisation shows that a company is healthy and stable. 'Large', however, starts at above $500 million!

Earnings per share (EPS) This is the company's yearly net profit spread across the number of shares on the market.

$5.8 million profit ÷ 2 million shares = $2.90 per share

With detailed follow-up this is a very useful tool, but be aware that the EPS can be distorted or misunderstood. High profits look good, but maybe new shares were released, inflating cash. Or profits could look weak, but maybe the company spent a lot of money preparing a new product, and profits will soar next year. Are these one-off events or a true indicator?

Price/earnings ratio (P/E or PER) This figure is the EPS compared to the share price.

$$\$2.50 \text{ share price} \div \$2.90 \text{ EPS} = 0.86$$

This means that it would take 0.86 years, or about ten months, to earn back the cost of the shares. If the company is healthy and debt-free, this is good. If the company has spent all its money this is a danger signal as it is an unrealistic expectation. Normal P/E ratios are much higher than this example.

Return on equity (ROE) This is net profit compared to the shareholders' funds. The shareholders' funds equal the total assets minus the total liabilities (these assets can include intangible items).

$$\$5.8 \text{ million profit} \div 2.5 \text{ million assets} = 2.32 \text{ per cent}$$

A company should have a high ROE, a little higher than the average current interest rate. This example isn't looking good for DarCom.

Dividend yield (DY) This figure is what you get back for owning the shares.

$$DY = 0.15 \text{ dividend} \div \$2.50 \text{ share price or } 0.06 \text{ (6 per cent)}$$

Every DarCom share yields a 6 per cent return. Dividends are lovely, but they are not always paid and the amounts change.

A big family budget

A company's financial information should look like a healthy family budget. The company should be spending efficiently and making a profit.

Technical tools

Technical analysis or charting is a large, detailed subject. Fortunately there are many good computer programs that will help you. Some of them combine fundamental and technical analysis, and offer a portfolio manager and other useful utilities. You can also update information online with some software.

A key area of charting is trends. Like the economy in general, the share market has different stages: top, down, bottom, and up. The market will move from one stage to another.

Knowing detailed information about the present stage helps predict general trends. Detailed info on specific shares helps the investor to know what to buy, when to buy, and how long to hold on.

Some of the programs listed below are free, others aren't. We're not making any specific recommendations, so visit the websites, download a demo and make a decision based on what suits you. Once you've found a program that works, stick with it. Having five different programs won't help you any more than just having one.

> www.click2.com.au/se (*ShareExpress2000* portfolio manager)
> www.InsightTrading.com.au (*Fundamental & Technical Manager*)
> www.tunwand.com.au (*StockMan* share program)
> www.saratoga.com.au (investment company, but has a virtual trading program for learning about investment)
> www.asx.com.au (the ASX site, which has many learning options)

Check your local software store for other programs.

Research recap

1   Choose a hot sector
2   List target companies
3   Run a fundamental analysis on each target
4   Run a technical analysis on each target
5   Weigh up the information, combined with any other sources
6   Choose a company
7   Decide your two per cent investment maximum
8   Decide your stop loss
9   GO!

Different methods of trading

Day trading

Many newcomers to share trading confuse *day trading* with *online trading*. Online trading involves making share trades over the Internet, usually through a discount broker (see *Choosing a broker*, page 144).

Day trading often uses the Internet and discount brokers too, but the day traders are actually very experienced professionals who watch the market constantly and make many fast and furious trades.

Day trading is something to aspire to, not something to start with. To be successful at day trading you need to be knowledgeable and experienced. Hold off until you've made some money, but by all means, take advantage of the Internet and discount brokers.

On/off market

There are other ways to trade shares besides the Australian Stock Exchange. Trading on the ASX is done via a broker and is called *on market*. But you can also trade *off market*, by approaching someone who either has shares to sell or wants to buy. It's a private negotiation and the shares are transferred from one party to the other using an *off-market transfer form*, available from the company or its share registry. A share registry is a list of shareholders and is available for a small fee to anyone who asks.

Some people make a lot of money trading shares off market. They approach the shareholders with an offer to buy shares; the shareholders simply sign the transfer form and get a cheque. Both parties save on brokerage fees. But be wary, sometimes the amount offered is well below the current trading price. Buyers count on unsophisticated shareholders to jump at the chance for cash and sell cheaply. If you receive an offer like this, check out the current share price before you do anything.

Some companies aren't listed on the Stock Exchange and *only* trade off market. If you're interested in an off-market company, contact them directly. They might have a facility for trading their shares, or they might be able to put you in contact with potential buyers and sellers.

Exempt market

This is another non-ASX market. It's not just off market, it's '*off-off market*', or a one company market. These are very rare and vary greatly. Contact the company directly.

Ex date vs record date

When buying or selling shares, be aware of various date restrictions. When a company pays a dividend, it sets a *record date*. This means that all those shareholders who hold shares on that date will get the dividend. This date is determined by the company and is usually a few weeks before the actual dividend payment date, but it can be anywhere from the day before to several months before.

If you purchase shares and the company is about to pay a dividend, purchasing them on the record date does not necessarily mean that you will be paid the dividend. There is a date called *ex date*. This is usually three working days prior to the record date. During the 'ex' period, anyone who sells shares will retain their right to the dividend, as there is a settlement period for transferring the shares from the buyer to the seller. This is called T+3, or trading date plus three days. So if you buy shares on Monday, they may not appear on the company's register until Wednesday.

If you want to buy shares to get a dividend, rights issue, or anything that requires having shares on the record date, make sure you buy them at least three days before the record date.

Leverage and gearing

In physics, leveraging means using a tool to multiply strength. In investing, it means using *other people's money* (OPM) to earn a profit. Like getting a loan — you may not have $150 000 for a house, but by striking a deal with a bank you can have a house now and pay back over a period of years.

Gearing is the overall process of using OPM to invest. Leveraging is the specific benefit of increasing power with borrowed money.

Many experts advise you to 'use OPM in *all* deals'. In real estate this is good advice. Why not use a loan to buy investment property? Your cash is tied up otherwise. But when it comes to shares, loans are dangerous. Real estate can probably be sold in an emergency, but shares could become toilet paper.

Even though it's quite risky, banks are fairly open-minded about lending money for share investment. They will lend you a specific amount, and the deal has to meet their standards. Generally banks don't like to lend over half the money for a deal, but they may go higher in some circumstances (real estate is usually 75 per cent).

It may be tempting to borrow money to get started in shares, but leveraging in shares is dangerous and may be a tool best left to experienced investors.

How to get started

Choosing a broker

You'll need a stockbroker (also called a *sharebroker*) to trade shares. It's the law for publicly listed shares. Full service brokers offer advice and charge about 1.5 to 2.5 per cent of the trade as a commission, with a $50 minimum fee. This is per trade, and applies to both buying and selling. This can easily wipe out any profits if you're a small investor.

The advice stockbrokers give is based on company analysis of the market and individual shares, and personal broking experience. The advice is often conservative, and despite their best efforts, it is not always correct. (Remember, there are no magic formulas!) But full-service brokers know their clients' individual strategies and situations, and they can be very helpful.

Discount brokers just make the trades, without offering advice. They are still a good resource for basic information, though — they don't refuse to speak except to take orders! They want you to be successful, but they can't recommend shares or tell you what to do. The charges vary between brokers and between phone trades and internet trades. You can expect to pay between $30 and $80, though some start at $10–15. An $80 fee sounds like a lot, but it isn't compared to the $300 you might pay as a percentage of a full-service trade. Online trading is definitely the cheapest option. Some of the larger banks offer online discount trading.

Brokers can be found in the *Yellow Pages* under 'Stock & Share Brokers'. Both full-service and discount brokers are listed.

Be aware that sometimes full-service brokers give biased advice. They have invested heavily in certain shares and they have an interest in keeping the share price healthy. Unscrupulous brokers will also list false bids to manipulate price. You have no way of knowing except to choose a reputable broker.

Learn to earn

The Australian Stock Exchange (ASX) offers share investment courses run by high-profile investment companies and brokers. You can ask questions and pick up some useful information. The courses are usually free, but they fill up fast so you need to get in quickly.

You can learn without losing by playing the ASX virtual trading game. You're given $50 000 in virtual cash and you can pick your own shares, just as if it were real. The games require registration and run for eight weeks. It's fun and it's great experience. See the ASX website (www.asx.com.au).

Another virtual trading game is by Saratoga Investments (www.saratoga.com.au), an investment group. They are in business to sell you their advice and services, but you can also download the trading game for free and learn how to trade.

By practising you'll get a good feel for the market — its

ups and downs, highs and lows — all without risking a cent!

The Small Business Show and Sunday Business are useful, as well as Business Review Weekly (BRW) magazine, Shares magazine and Personal Investor. Don't get bogged down in educating yourself, though; it is vital that you actually *start trading*.

REal EStatE

In medieval times, land was everything. The land produced food and materials. Feudal lords owned land and leased it to farmers. The farmers kept a small portion of the goods produced and the rest went to the landlord. It was good to be a landlord. Other people made money for you, *and* you charged them for using your land!

In modern times, land isn't quite so important. Technology and society make survival easy in the Western world. But it's still good to be a landlord.

Real estate is called 'real' because you can touch it. A business might lose its assets, shares may become worthless, but someone always wants space. As space becomes less available it becomes more valuable. A growing economy (including inflation) makes real estate prices go up. Sometimes prices go down, but real estate can give you a steady unearned income, keeping your money machine running smoothly.

There are three basic ways to invest in real estate:

1   Buy or build a property to rent out, either residential or commercial

2   Fix up a property to sell for more
3   Create a development from raw materials and sell.

Most investors start with the first option, usually buying an existing property. It's similar to buying a franchise in business: the groundwork is done. Expect to make between 5 and 10 per cent return on investment (ROI).

The second option is a great way to make a larger profit quickly. There's risk, but there's also a great profit-to-effort ratio: a little work can increase value greatly. Expect to make between 10 and 15 per cent ROI, though this does go higher.

The third option is for experienced investors. The projects are usually large, such as shopping centres. These aren't built because a local council thinks it would be convenient for shoppers; *developers* or business people see an opportunity to make money. They plan, pre-lease the shops, then buy untamed land cheaply and build. Sometimes they buy an old, rundown property, demolish it and subdivide the land.

Developing is risky and hard work, but the profit is good, about 25 per cent ROI.

Buying to rent out

If you follow time-tested methods you can expect to make 5 to 10 per cent profit on the average deal. A $200 000 property would earn you an average of $14 000 per year, or $270 per week. The ultimate plan is to have the rent pay for the investment mortgage with some cash left over, and then years later sell the property for a profit.

Many factors affect the ultimate plan. Location, tenants, general market, the conditions and interest on the loan, to name a few. With rental prices and mortgage rates, you're often forced into a long-term deal: the rent barely covers the mortgage and expenses, and you either break even or lose. Any real profit might only come when the property is sold. But that's not necessarily all bad (see *Negative gearing*, page 169).

Rental investment

As with all investments, you need a plan. Your plan can be altered, but you need a firm idea of what you want and how to get it. Start by buying one residential house and renting it to a family. Your goal is to sell the house years later for a profit.

Five years is about the minimum to own an investment property. It takes this long to make the venture profitable, and for the value to increase enough to make a profit when you sell. If you're making money, keep it longer.

You've got to work out what you can afford, where, and how much you can charge in rent, then estimate what it will be worth in five years. Look in the real estate section of the paper, get all the free real estate magazines, and start looking at houses. You're not looking to buy a home for yourself, you're buying a tool to feed your money machine. Don't be emotional. Find out where there's a demand for rental properties. Look at the average weekly rent. Now add up the numbers and see what you can roughly afford.

Example
$150 000 apartment
Loan repayments $190 per week
Rent you can charge $210 per week
Profit $20 per week

In this example you'd be making money. But you also have to allow for the cost of maintenance, managing the property (which includes collecting rent and paperwork), and of course, tax.

It might work out that you're barely making a profit at all. But then, someone is paying the mortgage for you, and you can *probably* sell the house for $160 000–165 000+ in five years. That would be a $15 000 profit (or maybe more).

House, shop, small or large

So what type of property should you buy? If you decide to start with residential property, you'll be looking at a unit or a house. Both have their pros and cons. Units can be cheap to buy and easy to rent out, but they won't increase much in value, and they won't bring in much rent (it's all about space). Houses can be maintenance monsters, but they sell for more. In residential property landlords pay rates but tenants pay utilities.

Commercial property is more expensive to buy than a house, but you'll save in other areas because tenants usually pay utilities, maintenance and rates.

The tenants from hell

Tenants and landlords often complain about each other. We'll assume most parties on both sides are fair, but there are some difficult tenants. The laws protecting tenants tend to be biased towards tenants, and as a landlord you can be in for some frustrating times.

Our friends rented out a house. The tenants destroyed the yard and the walls inside, and then they couldn't pay the rent. Eventually patience and kindness ran out, and it was time for the tenants to go. But they stalled and used the law to their advantage. Months passed and they wouldn't leave. Rent-free months with more damage added to the list. Finally the tenants were forcibly removed, but the damage bill was high.

How can you avoid a situation like this? Laws and

contracts offer some safety, but the best protection in any deal is a solid foundation. If you trust the people in business with you, then you'll probably be all right. Choose tenants carefully. It is illegal and unethical to discriminate based on race, gender or religion (to name a few restrictions), but it's perfectly acceptable to choose tenants who you think will pay on time and take care of the property.

Interview prospective tenants as if you were hiring them for employment. Do they make enough money to pay the rent? Do they have any unusual expenses? A couple making a combined income of $35 000 a year with 11 children probably couldn't afford to pay $240 a week in rent as well as feed and clothe the family.

Find out whether your applicants have permanent jobs. It's not unreasonable to ask to see their payslips. They're entering into a payment-based contract with you. Ask the types of questions a bank might ask when applying for a loan. Ask for a reference from a previous landlord and check with the residential tenancies institute in your State; they're listed under Consumer and Business Affairs in your local White Pages. They can tell you if a prospective tenant has been a problem in the past or has been blacklisted.

Do a house inspection report. You've probably seen examples of these in your own rental experience. Make up a list cataloguing each item in each room: floor coverings, light fittings, walls, etc. Photograph the property inside and out, then walk through with the tenant. Note the condition of every item in every room. Have the applicants sign the report and give them a copy. When it's time for them to leave, do another walk-through and compare. Some wear is normal, but damage is not. The report will make it easier to claim for damages or justify eviction.

Your residential tenancies institute has many forms

relating to the responsibilities and protection of the landlord. They are also involved in holding the security money (*bond*) you collect from the tenant at the beginning of the tenancy — usually one month's rent. It's not money for you — the tenants get it back when they leave. If there is any damage, or owed rent, you can take the money owed out of the bond.

Shops and factories

Instead of (or in addition to) residential property, you can buy commercial property, such as a small strip mall or industrial building. If you have a single building with room for one tenant (*single-tenant premises*), your job is easy, but if you own a small shopping centre with three or four shops (*multi-tenant premises*), you'll have to make the building attractive to tenants and to the public, because you need your tenant businesses to be successful.

Small strip malls are a bit risky. They only have a handful of small shops; no large tenants like Myer or K-Mart (*anchor* businesses, to use the lingo). If a tenant business goes under or moves to other premises, you've lost a huge percentage of income. But small centres are usually in a visible spot aimed at foot and car traffic, convenient for their neighbourhood. If tenanted well, they can be successful.

A medium or large multi-tenant building usually has 5 to 10 per cent of its shops empty at one time. These buildings can be more work, but they can also be safer. With lots of tenants and turnover, you can afford to lose a few businesses. Anchor businesses are safe. They're also powerful; because the anchors are so important to you, they can demand lower rent and special privileges.

Please re-lease me

Whether you're buying an empty building and looking for new tenants, or buying a fully tenanted property, the lease with each tenant is key. You might find a great building but no tenants, or maybe worse, existing tenants with leases that are no advantage to you — unreasonably long-term and possibly low-paying.

Write down everything you want in your ultimate lease. You want the tenants to pay you as much as possible without pressuring their business, and you want them to be responsible for as many expenses as is reasonable. You'll never get your tenants to agree to everything, but it's a starting point.

If you have existing tenants, they may be hesitant about changing the terms of the lease, but the new lease may be better for them, too. As with all business, the strongest and most efficient deals are the ones that are fair to both sides.

Potential problems in a lease include:

1   No penalty for late rent payment
2   Difficulty in evicting the tenant if obligations are not met
3   No rules of business behaviour
4   No future rent rises
5   Special situations or allowances that will upset other tenants

Some tenants may ask for something special. You can charge extra or negotiate a deal that suits both of you.

Rent and paperwork

Get a separate bank account for your real estate empire, even if you only own one property. You'll need to keep simple but accurate records for your safety, and for the Tax Office. And always give your tenants a receipt.

That's all there is to it. Find a property where the numbers work, get a tenant, and make money. The hard part is finding a deal that works; the scary part is taking the risk. The fun part is counting the money and watching your money machine work for you.

Renovating

Renovating and reselling property is an excellent way to make money. Buy a property that needs work but has great potential, fix it up so it *looks* great, and then resell it for a profit. This is often called *speculating*, because you're gambling on making a quick profit.

Why does this work? Because most people will pay a fair price (or even more) for a beautiful home. Some don't want to do the work, others look at a rundown house and think it's ready for the scrap heap because they can't visualise the potential.

The most important point to remember is to put in as *little effort and money* as possible. Don't fix or change anything that doesn't equal improved value. If you paint the front of the house, potential buyers see a pretty, 'new' house. They'll more pay for this. If you change the glass in the windows you're wasting your money (unless the windows were broken). You need to focus on the following:

Garden Chop out old/scraggly bits. Clean or paint concrete driveways. Plant colourful flowers and toss some mulch around. Don't spend thousands on mature trees or a new lawn, and don't worry about repaving; throw down some gravel instead. Most buyers will make changes anyway.

Façade This may sound like a quirky French restaurant, but it's just the face or front of the property. Don't worry so much about the rear or the sides, because the front is what people see first. Sometimes a bit of paint will be enough, especially on weatherboards. If the brick is daggy, paint or render it with concrete. The difference it can make is amazing; you can transform a dark 1970s house with arches into a trendy Spanish hacienda.

Repaint A new coat of paint costs little and adds a lot of perceived value. It can transform an old, drab house into a bright, new home. Use neutral colours; they make the house look clean and new, and they won't offend buyers. Remember, the paint isn't for you, you're not going to live in the house.

Repolish/recarpet Drab floorboards can become new with a quick sand and recoat. If the house has carpet, will a steam clean fix it? That's much easier and cheaper than recarpeting, and the new owners may recarpet anyway. But if the existing carpet is a 1970s orange or lime shagpile, recarpet in a neutral colour.

Fixtures It's a small expense to replace dated and old fixtures. If the curtains match the '70s shagpile carpet, get rid of them. You can leave the windows plain or get inexpensive, ready-made curtains. Some potential buyers will want to add their own style and won't mind doing the curtains themselves. If the oven and cook-top work, just give them a good clean. You can buy special appliance paint for touch-ups.

We'll let you in on a secret. The main two areas you'll need to make spiffy in a renovation are the bathroom and the kitchen. People love 'em. Obviously everyone uses both, and spends a lot of time in one of them (we mean the kitchen — it's a great 'hang-out' spot). These two rooms are where money spent equals increased value. But don't spend any more than $15 000 for a bathroom and $25 000 for a kitchen. Any more and you're just wasting money.

Work with what you have. Instead of ripping out an old 1920s bathroom and building a modern dream bathroom, *highlight* the '20s feel with some paint and inexpensive fixtures.

Go to estate sales. Often a family or trust will sell a house quickly when an elderly person dies. Sometimes the property is sold to break up a larger package. You can often get a bargain house. We're not talking about going to funerals and looking for potential houses (though some people actually do this!) There's nothing ghoulish about matching a buyer to seller, even in difficult circumstances.

Flip it!

There's another way to speculate without actually doing any renovation or spending any money at all. You don't even have to buy the house! It's called *flipping,* and it's a great way to make a quick buck.

There are two key elements to flipping, both of which are beyond your control. Luck is the biggest part. Timing is key. Here's how it works.

You find a property that's undervalued. It could need work, the seller could be in a hurry or desperate, or it could be an estate sale. You make an offer and secure the deal with a contract to purchase the property in 30 or 45 days, with no actual money down. Then you find a buyer. This is the bit that takes a *lot* of luck, or a lot of contacts. Once you've found a buyer, you sell them the right to buy the property at a discount.

For example, say you've found a house selling for $150 000 that you know will sell for at least $165 000 or more. You secure it with a contract and then find a buyer. You offer the buyer a $5000 discount. The buyer pays you $10 000, and then buys the house from the original seller for $150 000. The seller gets rid of the house, the buyer gets a discount, and you make $10 000. You have provided a service and have charged for it.

Flipping really does happen, but it's a matter of seeing and seizing an opportunity. There may be legal issues as well, so talk to a lawyer.

Developing

Developing is about turning raw potential into a finished product — a paddock becomes a $50 million shopping centre. It takes experience, resources, time and money. It's *not* for the new investor. But you can still do some small developing and here are a few examples.

The housing estate we live in was developed privately. Three friends bought 3 hectares of bush from the water department. They got council approval to turn it into residential blocks, cleared the land and made two small streets. Re-sculpturing took care of the excess dirt. They divided the land into 20 blocks and sold them all, rather than building houses. Less profit, but less work and risk. Their biggest expenses were having the roads sealed, and the council permit fees.

Nearby, someone bought an ancient, crumbling house on a large block. The house was demolished and the land subdivided into seven tiny blocks, each now selling for $100 000. The house and land cost $350 000, and the subdivision permit cost $15 000.

An acquaintance found some country land going cheap in a growing area. He did some research: the land had ten titles attached to it. It could be subdivided without major council paperwork or fees. He teamed up with a partner and a loan and bought it. They will sell ten blocks for $100 000 each ($1 million in total). The initial cost of the land was $200 000.

This is the sort of deal *you* can do! Just recognise and seize opportunities. And do your research. Make sure the land can be subdivided, and that it's zoned for the proper use.

What's the title?

There are two types of land titles, Torrens and strata. A Torrens title means one house per block, with minimal restrictions. A strata title means that the outside of a group of properties is common, with common utilities and plenty of restrictions. Often developers will build ten houses in a row on a strata title; it's practically the same effect as building a small apartment building. There are pros and cons for both landlord and tenant, and every situation is different.

Location, location, location

You've probably heard the old saying, 'The three most important things in real estate are location, location and location.' It's a cliché, but it's absolutely true.

Buy the worst house in the best street. Even clean and prosperous suburbs have one 'bad apple', or a house that's mediocre. A house can be repaired, or pulled down and rebuilt. It's harder to fix an old waste dump that's a long way from shopping and schools.

Check out the neighbours. You don't want to buy the almost-worst house in the street, next to a neighbour with four rusting car wrecks who plays heavy metal music all night. You'll have trouble renting and selling the property, and the value may be affected.

To get tenants (and a good return on your investment), look for properties close to shopping, services and schools.

No one wants to live so far away from everything that they need a cut lunch just to get the newspaper. The property should be walking or short driving distance to public transport, but not *directly* on a train or bus route. Try to be within one hour of the city centre.

The more land the better — it's not the house that will appreciate in value, but the land. Houses come and go with time, but dirt is dirt and more importantly, space is space. Look for older houses near the city, as they often have large blocks. These are capital growth gems.

Try to find a house with 'character'. Colonial style houses or cottages will always retain their value. Look at what the style trend is now, and find something like it or something that can be altered at minimum cost.

Views are important. Ocean, beach, hills or vales. If it's pretty and you can see a lot of it from the property, then you want it. Water is key, whether it's the ocean, a river or an artificial lake. Proximity to parks or reserves, or even golf courses, is also an asset.

Look for potential growth areas, such as new estates or areas where new shops and schools are being built. Anywhere that people will flock to. Get in before the growth occurs. Afterwards is too late; prices will be too high for it to be worth your while.

Look at the council's development planning agenda for the area. The agenda will show potential problems, such as a major highway that has been planned to go straight past the front door in five years' time. A highway can be good if it's *nearby* (better for commuting), but bad if it's so close the traffic rattles the windows.

Buy in a buyer's market, where there are more sellers than buyers and people are desperate to sell. An indicator of this is dropping house prices. Check the real estate ads and look for properties that aren't selling; each week they may be a lower price. You may have to wait for the cycle of supply and demand to come around, but it's worth it.

Other resources

Use all the resources you can; information is your greatest tool (provided you use it!)

> *Personal Investment Magazine*
> *Australian Property Investor Magazine*
> www.property.com.au
> www.realtor.com.au
> www.realestate.com.au
> www.reiaustralia.com.au
> Real Estate Institute publications — they can help you find a property, understand the legal issues, and provide info on fees such as stamp duty
> *Money* – the television program and the magazine

Real estate agents — it's all for the seller, baby!

Here's something a lot of people don't realise: real estate agents work for the seller (also called the *vendor*). The agents get a commission based on the selling price of the property. The higher the price, the higher the commission.

Real estate agents want to match buyers with the properties they list, but they may not have anything that suits you, so it's quicker and easier to look in the ads yourself. A glance will tell you which agencies have potentially good properties.

Real estate agents will show you a house and try to close the sale right in the driveway. Don't be pressured! You're looking for an investment property, a money-making tool, not a home. You won't be emotional and you will follow your plan. You need time to calculate and think.

Most agents will ask for an offer straight away. When you say you need to think about it, they'll counter with, 'What are your concerns? I can answer your questions right now.' Another oldie is, 'Don't wait too long, this is going fast. I'm seeing two other couples this afternoon ...' Rubbish! If it's going to sell instantly, why are they hard-selling it to you? And if you *do* lose out, so what? *There's always another property.*

If you think you need assistance finding a property, think about hiring a buyer's advocate. These professionals source properties based on your requirements and can represent you throughout the sale. They charge for their services, but their experience and advice can be well worth it.

Generally you'll need either a licensed conveyancer or solicitor to transfer the property from the seller to you. You can do it yourself, but there are a lot of legal details and it is safer to have it done by a professional.

A conveyancer or solicitor can also look over the contract and offer advice. And they can do research on property a lot more easily than you can. Take advantage of any professional advice you can get.

Inspections

Inspect a property thoroughly before you think about buying. You'll need a professional building inspector. They look for problems we don't even think about, and they can be held liable (to some degree) for not seeing vital points.

An inspection may cost you a few hundred dollars, but it can save you thousands. You don't want to buy a termite-infested, damp-ridden problem that's about to fall into that wonderful 'ocean view'. Obviously you should wait until you feel pretty sure about a place before you pay for a building inspection, though.

Building inspectors advertise in the *Yellow Pages*. Some are Housing Industry Association (HIA) members or Association of Building Consultants (ABC) members, and some have a builder's licence as well. The HIA can help you find a building inspector or arrange an inspection.

You should do your own inspection, too. There are other things to consider as a landlord — will the carpets need replacing? Are the appliances worn out? Will you need to renovate before you eventually sell? You won't be living there, but you still need it to be liveable. And you want to make sure it'll grow in value.

Don't rely on any 'inspection' your bank may do. They will only work out its monetary value; they don't thoroughly check for faults. (This is short-sighted on their part!) If you're building a house, bank inspectors only check to see if the building has progressed to a certain stage in order to make the next payment to the builder. They don't inspect the quality of the work.

Be cheeky. Ask the agent outright what's wrong with the house. If you make it plain you're still interested and only asking so you can prepare, they may even be honest.

Valuations

Always make sure a property is worth at least what you're paying for it, preferably more. You can hire a valuer, or you can do the work yourself. Look at other houses in the area that sold recently. Remember to compare apples to apples: the same number of bedrooms, similar features etc. Go to open inspections and get a feel for what the properties actually have. Look through the papers and check the asking price of similar houses, then find out what they actually sold for.

You'll also need to visit your local Land Titles Office. They handle land title and deed transfers. For a small fee (sometimes only $10–15) you can find out when a house was built, how much it cost, if it has been sold before, among other things. The council's Valuer-General will have listed the most recent valuation. Actually, there will be two figures; a *capital value* (CV) of land and buildings, and a *site value* (SV) of the land only. Armed with this information, you can easily determine if the asking price is reasonable, and you may gain negotiating power.

A professional valuer will do essentially the same thing, though they do have experience in assessing houses in a walk-through. Whatever sort of valuation you get, it's an *opinion only*. It's more legal than an *appraisal*, but you still can't hold anyone to it. You might pay more or less than the valuation, and there's no guarantee you can sell the property for the valuation price. The buying or selling price of anything is determined by supply and demand: what the buyer is willing to pay and what the seller is willing to take. In a buyer's market, properties will sell for under their value, and in a seller's market they will sell for much more than they are probably worth.

Going, going, gone!

Auctions can be very dangerous. They're a good way to sell, but they're *usually* a terrible way to buy. The entire idea is to have people compete against each other, forcing the price up, usually faster and higher than you can expect in a regular sale. Every situation is different, but here are some basic golden rules for buying at auction:

Inspect the property Once you've bid successfully it's yours; there's no getting out of it if you discover termites after the fact.

Inspect the papers The contract is available for inspection prior to and/or at the auction. Ensure that everything is to your satisfaction, as there's no 'cooling off' period at auction.

Decide on your maximum bid and stick to it No matter what. Think of this in the same way as setting a stop loss in shares. If you miss out on the property there'll be another one.

Unscrupulous agents and auctioneers sometimes break the law and put *dummy bidders* in the crowd, people who make false high bids to drive the price up, although this will become less common as legislation to outlaw the practice comes into force. Protect yourself by sticking to your maximum bid. *Never* pay more than you can afford or more than a property is worth. There's no cooling off period at auction, so if you can't get that extra financing from the bank, you're still responsible for paying up somehow. It's also bad business to pay too much — you've got to make a profit on the deal eventually.

Don't bid straight away; wait for the auctioneer to say 'going once, going twice ...' If the price is still within your pre-set limit, get in just before they say 'gone'. That way you know exactly who you're bidding against and can be reasonably sure you are close to the final price.

You can sometimes buy an auction property privately prior to the auction if the seller is willing. Approach the seller or agent and make an offer. They may accept it rather than risk not getting their minimum price at the auction.

Go to a few auctions and get a feel for the process. See if you can spot the investment bidders (they're calm and stop at their limit), and the emotional home-buyers (they're tied up in knots and often push beyond what they can spend).

Getting the money

Unless you've just won the lotto (and if you have, good on you for investing and not splurging it all), you'll need financing for your investment property. Everything in the *Mortgages* section earlier in this book applies, but there's some other information you may need.

If you've been following a budget and paying extra off your own mortgage, you'll have *equity* in your home. Equity is the difference between what you've paid on the loan and what you owe. Say your mortgage is $150 000, and you've paid off $50 000. That means you've got $50 000 equity in the home loan. In this example your equity equals what you've paid, but your equity can increase without ever paying a cent! Say prices go up and your home is now worth $195 000. The bank is only interested in what you owe, or $100 000. Your equity is now $95 000, not just the $50 000 you've paid off the original loan. You can pull that equity out again as cash (depending on your loan), or you can borrow against it.

Banks love equity. It means that if the house has to be sold because you can't afford it, they'll at least get what they're owed. Banks will also lend you more if you have equity. Normally when you buy a house they like to have a little elbow room, which is why most banks will only lend 80 to 90 per cent of the value of the property, sometimes only 75 per cent for commercial or investment properties. But if you have equity they might lend you 100 per cent. You won't have to save for a deposit, and you might be able to borrow enough to cover all fees and charges.

You might be thinking it's better to borrow *less*, not more, because the more you borrow the more you'll have to pay in interest. However, unlike interest on your home loan, investment loan interest is *tax deductible*. It's more efficient to pay more off your home mortgage and borrow plenty for the investment mortgage. Remember other people's money: it can be dangerous to borrow money for shares, but it's smart to borrow for real estate.

An *interest only* loan might help even more. You only pay interest, then at the end of the loan you pay the money you borrowed as a lump sum. When you sell the property you'll have enough to pay off the loan. You won't have equity, but you get a great tax break. Because payments are smaller (just interest), you can use the extra money towards your own home loan.

Split-purpose loans

You can combine your own home loan with an investment loan so you only have one repayment to worry about. The main problem with this is tax. The Tax Office isn't too generous about determining where one loan starts and the other ends when it comes to claiming the interest as a deduction. They're warning people to get independent legal advice before jumping into a split-purpose loan.

How much should I borrow?

You'll need to figure out how much you can borrow. You've got to be able to make the repayments even if the property is sometimes empty. If you're borrowing to speculate or renovate, you'll have to be able to cover the loan for however long it takes to sell the property. (Some banks have a special development loan that covers the renovating.)

Banks want you to succeed. If you're making money, so are they. Look at a bank as a potential partner, rather than as an enemy. Sit down with a bank advisor and get help to find the right loan for the right property. But you've got to do some work ahead of time. Add up all the fees and expenses (including maintenance, stamp duty, GST, council rates, water rates, and more) and take a detailed package to the bank.

Banks have a good idea of what you can expect to receive in rent, and how easy it will be to keep the property occupied. They often count the rent you collect as part of your ability to repay the loan; they may include 60–80 per cent of the rent as part of your income.

You might be able to negotiate on some of the loan fees. If you already have a mortgage with the bank, use this as leverage. Once you have the final figures, they'll tell you how much they're willing to lend, and this figure minus the fees will give you an idea of how much you can spend.

Decide if you want to have a variable or fixed interest rate. The same information and logic from the *Mortgages* section applies here.

If you don't have any equity in your own home you'll need up to a 25 per cent deposit. Be aware that some banks may charge more interest for investment loans, but shop around and negotiate. There's no reason to pay more if you don't have to. And you don't have to go to the same bank that holds your home mortgage. (You won't need to move your home loan either.)

Try to get the maximum repayment period for your investment loan, usually 25 or 30 years. The longer the term, the lower the repayments will be and the more tax-deductible interest you will pay. Some banks look at commercial buildings differently, though. They often expect a lump sum payment to pay off the loan in ten years, because they're afraid the building may depreciate quickly.

Be your own bank!

Both sellers and buyers can benefit from owner-financing, where the property owner acts like a bank. Why would you want to be like a bank? Because you get the interest from the buyer! A seller gets a lot of money, yet a buyer can save a lot.

As a seller, you'll collect the house price *plus* the interest. On a $150 000 house that could mean $230 000! The buyer simply pays you in instalments, covering principal and interest. You don't get a lump sum, but you get much more money overall. If you're proposing it as a seller, you might have to offer a slight discount as an enticement, either on the total price, interest rate or deposit amount.

As a buyer, you'll pay in instalments anyway, so you won't see a difference. But if you think you'll have trouble getting a loan from a bank you might be able to convince a seller to owner-finance.

It can be risky. Both parties should trust each other, and legal advice is wise.

Gearing

Gearing is borrowing to invest. As we explored in *Shares*, it's a tool to give you more power. Gearing is called different things depending on how well it's working.

Positive gearing is what everyone wants, but it's often difficult to make it work. It means you make a *positive cash flow*, or profit, on your investment. You borrow $150 000 to buy an investment property, take in $800 a month in rent, and your expenses (the loan payments, fees, maintenance, insurance etc.) are only $700, so you make $100 a month profit. (Although after tax that might only be $65.)

Neutral gearing means your losses equal your gains —

you break even. You still gain in a way though, because your tenant is paying off the investment loan for you, and later you can sell the property for a profit. It's not what you aim for, but it's comfortable and it's still considered a success in real estate.

Negative gearing means you lose money. Your rental income is $800 a month, but the loan is at a high interest rate, the maintenance is expensive, and you're spending $850 a month. So you're losing $50 a month.

The Tax Office isn't often generous, but they do give you a break for losing money on an investment property. The loss can be applied to any gains you've made, such as other investments or wages, so you pay less tax.

Because of this tax benefit, some investors *plan* to negative gear. It's really planning to lose; don't be fooled by all those advising negative gearing as a road to success. But if you buy a property and can't find a tenant, or a tenant moves out, then you might have to lose money for a while. Or maybe the deal is bad, you didn't do your homework, and now the numbers don't add up. Take the tax break!

Just remember that it's not smart to spend money to lose money, even with a tax break. It's much better to plan to profit. You have to make the same amount of effort, so you might as well get ahead if you can.

Expenses

When you are trying to decide how much to borrow, you'll have to consider more than just the purchase price. To name just a few expenses, you'll have: valuation, inspection, legal or conveyancing fees and loan application fees (plus stamp duty on the mortgage or the transfer of the deeds). You'll also need to think about insurance (it should cover you from the moment you sign the contract).

Then there are ongoing expenses, which are often tax-deductible because you incur them while trying to earn a profit. Expenses in this category include things like: rates (council and water), taxes, maintenance, management fees, insurance, cleaning, gardening, advertising the property for rent, collecting rent, administration etc. The list seems endless. This is the hard part of trying to estimate your profit.

Tax

Taxation is complicated. Every situation is different. Tax laws also change constantly. We highly recommend that you consult a financial or tax advisor, the Australian Tax Office (ATO), or all three.

The ATO has several publications dealing with investment properties. Contact your local Tax Office or a financial advisor to obtain a copy. Some useful publications are:

Guide to Capital Gains Tax
Guide to Depreciating Assets
Rental Properties

Knowing what can be claimed as deductions is key to your preplanning. Tax is a big part of estimating profit.

Can you manage?

Should you manage your real estate empire yourself, or pay someone? Every situation is different, but it's all about profit-to-effort. If you only have a few properties and you have some time on your hands, you can keep the records, collect the rent and do the property maintenance. If you have built a vast empire or just don't have time, then hire someone. It eats up profit, but it may be the only smart way to do business. It's all a balance.

The last word

Some of you may have skipped to the end for the juicy stuff. But if you've read the book you know that the number one secret to financial wealth is ...

... there isn't a magic formula!

There's no special investing method guarded by a secret society and passed on to a select few. But to remind you about some of the important points:

1 Investing is simple, but not easy (work at it)
2 Learning about money is important, but actually doing it is more important
3 You will make mistakes — learn from them
4 Large piles of money shrink — keep money working
5 You can actually do it — even the big scary stuff — but you have to start!

We saved this for last. It's not technical information, but it's no less important.

There's no need to be greedy.

If you do amass a huge pile of money that continues to grow and grow, good on you. We mean there's no reason not to share. This isn't a lecture on charity or karma, but a practical note: money breeds money. You'll make more money if you use your money.

Hire and use local tradespeople and businesses. The people you do business with are potential partners and information sources. Who knows what deals you'll do together? It's okay to share the pie if you all benefit.

One last thing. Do not be discouraged when the road gets tough, or think that it's impossible to start with no money. The greatest barriers to success are disbelief and putting it off. If you can't find a good deal, keep looking.

Good luck and good investing!

INdEx

ALSO BY LOTHIAN BOOKS

Real Estate Myths Exploded
By David Morrell
RRP $24.95
ISBN 0 7344 0719 X

This is the book that estate agents don't want you to read!

Finding the right property takes time, care and experience. At all turns the buyer is confronted by people who, quite reasonably, want every last dollar they can get for their property. Whilst vendors have an agent acting on their behalf, the buyers have to go it alone, often falling prey to the sneaky tricks of estate agents.

Exposing the secret practices used by estate agents to boost sale prices, *Real Estate Myths Exploded* offers practical advice and hints on how to get the best possible price for the sale or purchase of your property.

David Morrell is a successful estate agent and auctioneer. Together with Christopher Koren, he founded Morrell & Koren, Australia's first buyers advocacy agency. He is famous for gate-crashing auctions and publicly exposing the unscrupulous and deceptive tactics used by agents. He has been profiled in the *Daily Telegraph*, *Australian Financial Review*, *Sunday Age*, *Sydney Morning Herald*, *Business Review Weekly* and the *Herald Sun*. He saves tens of thousands of dollars for his clients every year.

To order please visit your local bookstore
and quote the ISBN 0 7344 0719 X
or telephone toll free 1300 135 113

ALSO BY LOTHIAN BOOKS

Get Organised!
A practical guide to organising your home and office
By Carol Posenor
RRP $24.95
ISBN 0 7344 0331 3

Being organised comes naturally to some — but for others it is definitely a struggle. In our time-poor society it is easy to become weighed down by the chaos and confusion of a disorganised environment.

This practical book contains helpful advice and trade secrets to help you organise the two most important parts of your daily life — your office and your home.

Get Organised provides:

- ✔ the basic rules of becoming organised
- ✔ advice on choosing the best organisation systems
- ✔ guidelines on planning your space
- ✔ room-by-room advice on de-cluttering your home and work environments
- ✔ useful checklists throughout.

Carol Posenor is the managing director of Get Organised, a consultancy providing clients practical support to help them de-clutter their lives and keep themselves organised. She previously worked in banking and stockbroking where she identified a desperate need in many office environments to de-clutter, streamline and establish systems.

**To order please visit your local bookstore
and quote the ISBN 0 7344 0331 3
or telephone toll free 1300 135 113**

ALSO BY LOTHIAN BOOKS

Take Action!
Successful Australians share their secrets
By Yossi Segelman
RRP $24.95
ISBN 0 0 7344 0612 6

This amazing collection of stories features the personal stories of Australian celebrities, athletes, entrepreneurs, entertainers and politicians — all candidly revealing the secrets of their success.

Contributors include: Natalie Bloom, Bob Carr, General Peter Cosgrove, Alexander Downer, Lindsay Fox, Wendy Harmer, Marcia Hines, Lisa Ho, Akira Isogawa, Alan Jones, Ian Kiernan, Michael Klim, Sophie Lee, Quang Luu, John McGrath, Harry M. Miller, Kieren Perkins, Richard Pratt, Julia Ross, John Symond, Carla Zampatti and many more.

Yossi Segelman draws upon these stories to offer practical and inspiring solutions for those who want to change their lives.

Rabbi Yossi Segelman was born in London to a family of academics and educators, and is known as the 'corporate rabbi' for his work in business, event management, procurement and marketing. He is a consultant to organisations and businesses, specifying in lectures and giving advice on how to take action to achieve your maximum potential.

To order please visit your local bookstore
and quote the ISBN 0 7344 0612 6
or telephone toll free 1300 135 113